The Money Managers

THE
MONEY
MANAGERS

Professional Investment
Through Mutual Funds

Investment Company Institute

McGRAW-HILL BOOK COMPANY
New York
Sidney
Toronto
Johannesburg
London

THE MONEY MANAGERS

Professional Investment Through Mutual Funds

Library of Congress Catalog Card Number: 67–16303

First Edition

32010

Foreword

Our objective in preparing this book was to produce an interesting and factual work on mutual funds.

I believe that this objective has been attained. *The Money Managers* is not intended to be a definitive technical treatise on mutual funds, nor is it a passport to instant affluence. Rather, the book is a highly readable, authoritative reference work for anyone who wants to understand mutual funds—how they operate, what can and cannot be expected of them, and the place of the mutual fund industry in the economic scheme of things.

It is gratifying to me that this book was prepared at the time that I was President of the Investment Company Institute, and that I was able to make some small contribution to it. However, actual credit for it belongs to those people in the industry who contributed generously from their practical experience and devoted long hours of intensive work to the editorial task. Without the cooperation of the industry itself, and of the research staff of the Institute, the book could never have seen the light of day.

A book of this kind is long overdue. I commend it, and those who prepared it. They have made an important addition to modern financial literature.

DORSEY RICHARDSON

Contents

Foreword

Part One—The Money-Managing Machine

1.	The Need to Invest	3
2.	People and Premises	12
3.	The Mechanics of Money-Making	21
4.	The Risk-Reward Spectrum	28
5.	A Diversity of Uses	36
6.	The Cost of Services Rendered	45
7.	Purpose and Performance	56

Part Two—The Money Managers at Work

8.	The Rational Investment	73
9.	From Data to Decision	87
10.	Beyond Investment	98
11.	The Sale of Shares	103

Part Three—Money and the Marketplace

12.	Safeguards for Shareholders	111
13.	Economic Impact	120
14.	Funds and the Future	129

Bibliography	137
Index	143

The Money Managers

Part One

THE MONEY-MANAGING MACHINE

The Need to Invest

Jonathan Holdeen, a cash-conscious lawyer from Pine Plains, New York, once calculated that a single penny invested at 4 per cent compound interest would grow into $1000 trillion in the span of a thousand years. Acting on this flash of insight, Holdeen proceeded to create five thousand-year trusts. He also set up one—a short-termer, as it were—intended to endure for a mere five hundred years.

Holdeen's five thousand-year trusts, if they were to go all the way, would accumulate the modest sum of $9,988,380,000,000,000. This, for those who care to know, is $10 quadrillion, or about 17,000 times the entire gross national product of the U.S. today. The five-hundred-year "quickie," in which Holdeen invested $1 million, would have grown so large by the year 2444 that, in the nervous words of an internal revenue official, it would have "destroyed the tax base of the nation." Such, it would seem, is the power of investment.

How Mr. Holdeen's heirs make out in the future remains to be seen, but the story is of more than whimsical interest because it illustrates, in an extreme way, the

[3]

American urge to invest. Not everyone looks quite so far ahead, and few have enough money to tuck away several million for a far-off rainy day as Holdeen did, but Americans do save and invest in astronomical amounts.

The total sum saved or invested by Americans passed the trillion-dollar mark in 1961; it is over $1.4 trillion today. This unlikely figure includes the financial assets of individuals, partnerships, trust funds, and nonprofit institutions. It does not include such nonfinancial assets as jewelry, houses, and cars. In 1965 alone, savings in one form or another topped $34 billion, which worked out to roughly $7.50 out of every hundred dollars of take-home pay.

This is a lot of money in aggregate. It forms a mighty river whose tributaries branch out in many different directions. Some savers, of course, forego investment altogether and stuff their money into the traditional mattress. Others simply deposit it in the bank. There are those who invest in safe low-interest government bonds. Still others buy life insurance policies that increase in cash value over the years. Another group—about 20 million at latest count—buy shares of stock in corporations. Some buy real estate or lend out their money in the form of mortgages. Some speculators prefer to put their extra cash into Broadway shows, Impressionist paintings, or rare coins. Some favor still more exotic or volatile investments, ranging from puts and calls to Scotch whisky futures.

The list above only begins to suggest the varied ways in which money can be put to work in the increasingly complex U.S. economy. In fact, according to *Fortune* magazine, "the big news about investments these days is not just the increase in 'investable money,' but the extraordinary proliferation of new investment outlets, all of them offering different kinds of opportunities for different kinds of individuals."

Nevertheless, for millions of Americans today the four chief channels of investment are savings deposits, life insurance policies, bonds, and common stocks. Unfortunately, none of these is perfect.

The ideal investment, it has been said, is one that yields a high return at no risk, offers promise of substantial growth, and is instantly convertible into cash if money is needed for other purposes. This ideal specimen, of course, exists only in the fevered imagination of inexperienced investors. In the cold, hard market place each form of investment has its own special virtues and failings.

Savings deposits, for example, offer liquidity and a virtual absence of dollar risk. Barring catastrophe, the depositor can walk up to the teller's booth, present his passbook, and walk out with cash in hand. Despite compound interest, however, bank deposits grow slowly. In fact, interest rates sometimes lag behind the rate of inflation and what the saver receives at the end of the line is a fixed dollar sum that may actually be worth less in purchasing power than when set aside. The bank depositor trades off growth potential for fixed dollar safety.

Ordinary life insurance policies are more complicated. The purchaser pays a premium to the insurance company. Part of this buys him a guarantee that the company will pay a stipulated sum to the beneficiary upon the death of the insured. The rest of the premium is invested by the company for the customer. Thus the purchaser, as a rule, can turn in his policy and get some part of his money back. He can also borrow against the cash value.

In its investment approach, however, the insurance company is extremely conservative, so that the cash value

of the policy increases at what often seems an impercepti-
ble rate. As protection, an insurance policy is vital; as an
investment, it offers relative safety but slow growth.

Common stocks are likewise far from ideal. The stock
market has been called a place where a lot of good buys
turn into farewells, and American folklore is rich in similar references to peril in the securities market place.
Despite this, by 1966 more than one out of every ten
Americans owned shares of stock. This gave them equity—
ownership interest—in one or more corporations.

The virtue of common stocks is simple. They grow in
value as the company they represent grows, and, in an
expanding economy, not only have corporate earnings
grown, but the market has also been willing to pay a
higher price for each dollar of earnings. As a result,
common stocks have increased in value faster than inflation could chip away at the dollar. In the words of Dorsey
Richardson, a former president of the Investment Company Institute, "Inflation has depressed the purchasing
power of the dollar from a base of 100 in 1939 to approximately 45 cents today. Against this inflationary erosion of
purchasing power, common stock shares have generally
been regarded as affording some measure of protection."

Yet stock ownership can be risky. The investor has to
pick and choose among some 25,000 different publicly
traded stocks. The shares of these stocks, like particles
inside the atom, are in constant flux—rising and falling in
value, changing hands, and fluctuating in the amount of
dividends they pay. They are bought and sold in an
atmosphere superheated with gossip and uncertainty.
And the investor, even if he has chosen his portfolio well
and bought it at advantageous prices, must mount careful
day-by-day watch over it, for prices fluctuate incessantly.

Bond ownership also presents special problems. While high-grade corporate bonds, as well as U.S. government and municipal bonds, offer a high degree of assurance of being retired at face value and of paying a fixed rate of return until then, their prices fluctuate as the general level of interest rates changes. The bond buyer must consider the relationship of interest rates on corporate bonds relative to those of government and municipal bonds. He has to take into account the rate of inflation in the economy, the maturity date of the bond, and many other factors. And, of course, he is still faced with the job of selecting the right bonds from among those available in the market.

Because these four investment media offer such different results, many financial counselors argue that an individual needs a combination that provides a pool of ready cash in a savings account; some form of life insurance protection; and a portfolio of corporate securities (stocks and/or bonds) carefully selected and closely watched. Indeed, many securities dealers and brokers discourage customers from trying to invest in securities until they have both a savings account and life insurance coverage.

Of these common forms of investment, the greatest potential reward for the investor is found in the ownership of corporate securities. This investment area, however, is also the most complex and demanding.

Fortunately, ways have been devised to simplify the selection and supervision of a portfolio while reducing the risks ordinarily associated with the ownership of securities. One such approach is based on the mutual fund idea.

Mutual funds are not appropriate for everyone. They do not represent a panacea. They do not—despite a popular misconception to the contrary—eliminate risk. But they do offer an increasingly wide range of services to the investor. They have been so successful in recent years that, according to Arthur Wiesenberger & Co., a leading authority on investment companies, they "almost certainly qualify as the fastest-growing investment medium in the United States—and very likely in the entire world."

The mutual fund concept can be described simply. Shareholders in a fund, in effect, pool their money and hire professionals to buy and sell securities for them. If the professionals choose well and the securities in the portfolio rise in value, the value of each share rises in proportion. The fund, in the meantime, after deducting operating expenses, passes along to the shareholders substantially all dividends and interest that it receives from companies represented in its portfolio. It also distributes any profits that it may net from the purchase and sale of portfolio securities.

This system has three key advantages:

1. By pooling resources, the fund is in a position to diversify broadly. Instead of buying shares of General Motors alone, as the individual investor might do, it buys shares of perhaps 100 or 150 different companies in different types of industries, so that the investors' fortunes do not ride on a single company. This has the effect of spreading and reducing the risk of investment.

2. The fund relieves the individual investor of the need to select from among thousands of stocks on the market. In effect he turns that responsibility over to the professionals engaged by the fund. In addition, he need no longer keep daily tabs on his investment. The professional staff monitors the market place for him.

3. Because the fund stands ready to buy back its own shares at any time, the investor or his broker never has to

hunt up a buyer. The investment is almost as liquid as a bank deposit. The investor can get the current value of his investment in cash quickly if he needs it. Depending upon circumstances, of course, the amount he receives may be more or less than his cost.

Mutual funds offer a number of secondary advantages, but these three—diversification, professional management, and liquidity are the central ones. And so useful have these been that the industry, first formed about forty years ago, has shot up spectacularly as more and more Americans have learned of its existence. From spindly beginnings it has grown today to more than 375 funds. These invested an aggregate of $35 billion on behalf of more than 3,940,000 investors in 7,700,000 investor accounts at the end of 1966.*

Mutual funds, in fact, have grown so large that of the twenty-five largest companies in the United States, in terms of numbers of shareholders, ten are mutual funds. The biggest U.S. fund had $2.9 billion of assets invested on behalf of its shareholders in mid-1966.

Impressed by such statistics, financial columnist William Doyle has written: "The nation's mutual funds . . . are accepted as really big boys of the financial

* These figures do not include the holdings of "closed-end" investment companies, which are sometimes confused with mutual funds. The closed-end investment company issues shares and invests the proceeds in the securities of other corporations. Its own shares are bought and sold on the open market like those of any ordinary corporation. It does not offer shares to the public continuously. It does not promise to redeem or buy back its shares. The price of its shares may or may not at any given time reflect the current value of the securities it, in its turn, holds in its portfolio. Assets of active, diversified, publicly owned closed-end investment companies were $2.4 billion on December 31, 1966.

world. They no longer have to 'prove themselves.' . . . They are no longer Wall Street's stepchildren. They are now a potent factor in the nation's economy." And John Brooks in *The New Yorker* tells a similar story: "The mutual fund business has mushroomed so rapidly since the end of the Second World War that its growth has come to be compared to that of the life-insurance business a generation ago."

The story is dramatically confirmed by these figures:

Year-end	Number of accounts	Mutual fund assets
1940	300,000	448,000,000
1945	500,000	1,284,000,000
1950	950,000	2,531,000,000
1955	2,100,000	7,838,000,000
1960	4,900,000	17,026,000,000
1965	6,700,000	35,220,000,000
1966	7,700,000	34,829,000,000

This growth works out to roughly 20 per cent per year compounded, making the mutual fund business one of the nation's top growth industries. Sales of mutual fund shares amounted to $4.7 billion in 1966.

Yet the scope of fund activity cannot be gauged from these figures alone, for the funds, as noted, also buy and sell the shares of other companies. In all, funds currently account for the purchase and sale of $75 million worth of securities on an average day.

Most important for the individual shareholder, however, is the fact that the industry in 1966 distributed more than $875 million in dividends to shareholders. In addition, it paid out another $1318 million in the form of capital gains. This represented profits realized by the funds, on behalf of their shareholders, from the purchase and sale of portfolio securities. Thus the mutual fund industry in total distributed $2193 million from these two sources to its shareholders in 1966 alone.

Before we proceed to examine the mutual fund idea in greater detail—explaining, among other things, how funds work, how much they charge for their services, and how well they perform in the market place—let us look at the shareholders—the men and women who have made mutual funds "the fastest-growing investment medium"—and ask "Why do they use this particular form of investment?"

People
and
Premises

*Chapter
Two*

I WAS TWENTY-EIGHT when I first went
to work for the New York Stock Exchange," said a former
vice-president of the Exchange recently. "By the time I
was in my early thirties, I had a growing family, a new
house, and I found the only way I could hope to build an
equity estate was to put some money aside regularly out
of my salary. I also realized that even though I was an
officer of the Exchange, I was so busy I had little time to
devote to my own personal financial affairs. I soon found
I was turning to mutual funds."

The man who told this story ultimately went on to work
for a mutual fund, and is today the president of one of the
country's giant funds. He still invests in mutual fund
shares.

What is important here is not that someone connected
with a fund buys shares; many fund executives invest
exclusively in mutual fund shares. What is interesting is
that this anecdote dramatically illustrates a minor revolution on Wall Street.

Mutual funds have developed in a way that is a complete reversal of the usual financial pattern. Common
stocks for many years were thought to be safe for rich and
sophisticated investors only. It was not until after World

War I that people of modest means began to buy stock—
the poor followed the rich into the stock market. In the
case of mutual funds, it was the small investor who led
the way. He did so with such confidence, and the results
on balance were so salutary, that larger investors and
financial sophisticates—including officials of brokerage
firms and stock exchanges—have followed in his path.

Mutual fund ownership has now spread through a cross-
section of the American population. Fund shares have
been bought by golf pros, Hollywood movie queens,
lawyers, tax men, salesmen, executives, to say nothing of
political figures. Not long ago Vice-President Hubert
Humphrey publicly praised mutual funds and pointed out
that he had himself invested in them. Mutual fund investors come in all sizes, shapes, and colors. Some are
manual laborers struggling to put a few dollars aside.
Others are millionaires.

Why do these people save?

According to the Survey Research Center of the University of Michigan, "Families have a wide variety of
reasons for saving. Families with incomes of $7500 and
over tend to report the long-term objectives of retirement
and of children's education somewhat more frequently
than do those with lower incomes. Half of all the reasons
given by families with under $3000 income fall into short-
term categories of illness, emergencies, unemployment,
etc."

These findings jibe with the results of a 1966 study by
the Investment Company Institute. The Institute found
that the most frequently cited investment objective of
mutual fund shareholders was the creation of future retirement income. More than 60 per cent of all shareholders gave this as a primary reason for owning mutual

fund shares. More than 50 per cent said they were concerned about protection against inflation. Education for their children was given as the motivation for investment by between 23 and 35 per cent.

The accent on retirement income reflects the fact that Americans can expect to live longer and retire earlier in the years to come. Their concern about the future is well warranted, for most Americans face a severe jolt when job income ends. Social security was never intended to do more than supplement retirement income from other sources, and even though federal payments have been increased, the total is still far below what is necessary to provide for a decently comfortable old age.

The problem was perhaps first put in perspective a few years ago by William J. Casey, author of a number of personal investment guides. Casey argued, "The big new fact of financial life today is that it takes a six-figure sum, $100,000 give or take a little, to provide a man in retirement or his family at his death a substitute income sufficient to maintain a reasonable living standard."

He arrives at this conclusion in the following manner: "It is projected that in 25 years . . . the average American household would have an annual income of $13,000. If the dollar continues to lose value at two per cent a year, it will take $20,000 to buy a $13,000 living standard in 1982. But let's be very conservative. Let's allow for over-optimism. Let's hope inflation can be curbed. Let's suppose that, in retirement, it will be possible to live on half rations. On the basis of all these happy assumptions, let's cut the target down to $6000 a year, and let's suppose social security will take care of 30 per cent of that. At three per cent savings bank yield, it will still take over $150,000 of capital to do the job." Interest rates may fluctuate; they have risen since this was written. Yet Casey's point is well taken.

A leading Boston fund distributor makes a similarly dramatic point another way. He cites estimates of the American Medical Association on increasing life expectancy at age sixty-five. "The money you will spend if your retirement years are extended is really quite staggering," he points out. "For instance, if you plan to spend $400 monthly ($4800 a year), the total spent from age 65 to 80 would be $72,000. If you retired at 62 and lived to age 90, the total would be $134,000."

Whether or not the average mutual fund shareholder has stopped to figure all this out, it is clear that he spends a good bit of time worrying about the day he will stop receiving his paycheck.

Similarly, as we have seen, the problem of educating their children looms large among younger investors. According to the American Council on Education, it cost between $2900 and $3800 to send a child to one of twenty large public universities in the early 1950's. This figure covered four years of tuition, fees, and room and board. By the early 1960's the amount of money needed had soared to $4400 to $6000. At private universities, the comparable figures rose to from $4900 to $9100.

Moreover, college costs are still rocketing skyward. Rexford G. Moon of the College Entrance Examination Board has predicted that by the late 1970's they will reach $12,480 for four years at a state university and more than $20,000 at a private school. None of these figures includes such additional expense items as books, clothing, travel, allowance, and the like. A family with three children may thus face a college-education bill amounting to about

$25,000 today and as much as $60,000 in the late 1970's. A substantial group of mutual fund shareholders are justifiably concerned about this trend and are trying to do something about it.

Of course, the reasons for saving are as varied as people themselves. Yet retirement and education are the two major themes heard again and again.

Let us go back now to the question of who these savers or investors are. In general, everything said above tends to confirm the popular conception of the mutual fund shareholder as a small investor. Yet a surprising trend has begun to show up on the sales charts of funds all over the country: the tendency toward larger and larger average sales.

In the words of *Business Week,* "You'll soon be hearing more about a change in the profile of the mutual fund buyer. Most of the big, active mutuals now report that they are selling shares in bigger packages to people with bigger bankrolls."

A vice-president of one of the older funds has said: "It's remarkable that in the last few years the average size of our holdings has gone up dramatically. In the past year, about 40 per cent of all our sales were in units of $25,000 or more. This is most unusual as compared to 10 years ago."

Another fund states: "Investor purchases of $10,000 or more . . . accounted for more than half of the year's sales volume. This pattern contradicts the once-popular belief that mutual funds are only for the 'little' investor."

Still another fund has listed among its individual investors a man whose holding equals $1 million and a woman whose account holds $340,000. And one fund claims 860 investors each of whom holds an account worth more than $100,000. Together these 860 own $120,-300,000 worth of shares in the fund.

While there is a tendency for more and more knowledgeable and sophisticated investors of substantial means to become mutual fund shareholders, the backbone of the industry will always be people of moderate means.

At any rate, the increase in average sale volume is directly related to still another type of investor—the institution.

Charles P. Wesner is the president of Litho Color Plate Company in Minneapolis. He employs thirty-two people, most of whom are covered by a union contract. For the managers and supervisors who are not covered Wesner some years ago set up a pension fund. His problem was a common one: how to invest the pension fund money. After talking with the trust officer of a bank and a salesman for a mutual fund, Wesner decided the money would grow faster in the mutual fund. Starting with a few thousand dollars eight years ago, the pension fund value has now increased to more than $100,000, as a result of both additional investment and appreciation. According to Wesner, "We looked into mutual funds and found that with the investments they make and the capable people that follow and check all the different stocks on the market, this offered better protection for our money."

The use of mutual funds in this way is not limited to small business. Mobil Oil Corporation, for example, as one alternative in a plan intended to offer employees additional retirement income, will match sums invested by its employees in mutual fund shares.

Businesses, however, are not the only institutional investors. A survey of seventy-four mutual funds conducted by the Investment Company Institute showed that, as of the end of 1966, these funds held over 700,000 accounts on behalf of institutional investors. Of these, 637,701 accounts belonged to banks or individuals serving as trustees, guardians, and estate administrators. Another 13,000 belonged to business corporations. Apart from these, there were 16,500 accounts held by employees' pension and profit-sharing funds. Some 379 labor unions held an aggregate of over $15 million in seventy-four mutual funds. And thousands of accounts were held by churches, voluntary organizations, hospitals, schools, and colleges. All told, these seventy-four funds had $4.0 billion in institutional accounts. This represented 14.3 per cent of their total assets.

The growing tendency of large institutional investors to buy mutual fund shares is explained by one fund official this way: "The large investor knows that the era has probably long since passed when an individual could simply buy the common stocks of a dozen or so good companies and hold them indefinitely with some justifiable expectation that his investment would be profitable."

The thinking of many institutional mutual fund shareholders is perhaps best expressed by a letter dated October 22, 1964, written by the Rev. Gervase J. Soukup, Ph.D., comptroller of St. John's University, a small Catholic institution in Collegeville, Minnesota. It was addressed to the financial secretary of a labor union in Beaumont, Texas, who had written requesting information about the University's experience with a certain mutual fund in which it had invested pension funds for its faculty.

"I would certainly undertake a program of education of

your membership and sell them on a mutual fund approach," wrote Father Gervase. "For example, it could be shown them that our original investment in ———— Fund, made in May of 1957, has shown a market appreciation of 55.5 per cent. This means that today we could get $155,500 for the original $100,000 we put in the fund. In addition, the fund has been paying us dividend income . . . if one of our professors were to retire at this time, his pension, monthly, would be 31.4 per cent more than he thought it would be when we first began our plan. Conceivably, if this market—and the economy—keeps on growing and prospering, a pensioner, upon retirement, may be receiving several times the benefits he initially thought he would receive."

The letter goes on to explain some of the mechanics of the faculty pension plan and concludes:

Our past experience does not in itself guarantee that [the mutual fund] may do better. . . . As an economist, I'm sure that as a nation we are committed to a policy of full employment and continued high levels of economic growth. . . . So we will continue to have higher wages, higher levels of income, higher profits—and all this spells higher stock prices, perhaps continued but mild inflation. Surely no deflation. Therefore, why not put a pension fund in a variable dollar situation, rather than a fixed dollar investment, such as insurance?

You might get the idea from the above that I'm a fund salesman. I'm not, but I do teach a few upper division college courses in Investments and Finance, and I'm sold on investment trust funds [mutual funds]. . . ."

For both individuals and for institutions, mutual funds have proved valuable. They have done so because of their unique structure and method, which make possible not only professional management and diversification but also high liquidity. It is a structure and an approach that is highly flexible, easily adaptable to the varying needs of different classes of investors. To understand the services funds offer, it will help if we first ask "What exactly is a mutual fund?"

The
Mechanics
of
Money-Making

Chapter
Three

A MUTUAL FUND is a financial service organization that receives money from shareholders, invests it, earns returns on it, works to make it grow, and agrees to pay the shareholder cash on demand for the current value of his investment. Sometimes this service fails to perform as intended. Mutual fund shareholders can—and sometimes do—lose money. On the whole, however, the mutual fund system of investment has performed extraordinarily well for forty years. It has been refined and adapted in various ways since its invention, but the basic design has remained essentially unchanged. For anyone interested in mutual funds, or even in the general character of American finance, an understanding of this system is useful. Let us strip the mutual fund system to its bare essentials and see how it works—and why.

The mutual fund is, typically, a corporation. As such it issues shares. Most ordinary corporations and closed-end investment companies issue a fixed number of shares and do not continuously offer them to the public. Most mutual funds do offer shares to the public continuously. They issue new shares every day—as many as anyone is willing to buy. Because they issue shares continuously and redeem them continuously, they are "open-ended" and, indeed, the technical term for a mutual fund is an "open-end investment company" or "open-end investment trust."

The price of a mutual fund share is arrived at differently than the price of the shares of any other kind of corporation. When an investor wants to buy a share of stock issued by an ordinary corporation—United States Steel, for example—he or his broker usually must buy that share from someone else who already owns it. The purchase of the share represents a transfer from one shareholder to another.

The price Investor A pays Investor B for this share will depend in large measure on the popularity of United States Steel stock at that moment. If investors are clamoring for shares of United States Steel, the price will rise. If buyers are scarce and Investor B wants to unload his share, the price will naturally decline. In short, the price of a share of the stock of any ordinary corporation fluctuates with the stock's popularity among investors.

This is not the case with mutual fund shares. When an individual buys a share of a mutual fund, he buys it not from another investor but from the fund itself. And when he wishes to sell his share (in mutual fund terminology, "redeem" it), he does not sell to another investor but back to the fund itself.

The fund guarantees to buy back all shares of its own stock. As a result, the price of these shares is unaffected by supply and demand. The fund supplies all the shares needed, and it buys back all those offered for sale by its shareholders. The price thus does not fluctuate in direct response to popularity, gossip, rumor, or other extraneous factors.

What *does* determine the price of the share, then? The answer is the value of the fund's portfolio. As the fund receives money from its shareholders, it buys the securities of other corporations for its portfolio. Twice each day —at midday and at the close of business—the typical fund calculates the exact dollar value of each of the securities in its portfolio. Adding all this plus other assets (cash, etc.)—minus liabilities, of course—gives the fund the aggregate worth of its holdings, called its "net asset value." This figure is then divided by the number of shares of the fund held by its own stockholders. The result is the net asset value per share. And, if we leave aside for the moment the question of commissions, charges, or fees (see Chapter Six), this net asset value per share determines the price at which the fund both sells and buys its own shares.

Roughly speaking, therefore, if a fund owns a portfolio of corporate stocks worth $100 million, and the fund itself has sold 10 million shares of its own stock to the public, the net asset value of each mutual fund share held by the public would be $10.

Now let us say that, since the first of this year, the same fund has issued another 5 million shares of stock to the public and received in return an additional $50 million in new capital from its shareholders. It invests this money for them. As the money comes in it keeps on buying corporate securities and its portfolio gets bigger and bigger. In effect, the fund becomes a part-owner of each of the corporations represented in that portfolio—which may include shares of as many as 100 or 200 different companies. And at any given time the price of the mutual fund share continues to reflect the value of its portfolio.

Up to now, the mutual fund shareholder has paid

money into the fund. Now he begins to receive money back. Since most of the corporations represented in the fund's portfolio declare dividends at regular intervals, the fund, as a shareowner in these corporations, receives dividend income. It may also receive interest on its bond holdings. This income the fund distributes proportionately among its own shareholders after paying its expenses.

In this sense, the fund serves essentially as a pipeline for dividends and other income. Its ownership of a portfolio of corporate securities entitles it to collect dividends and interest from the corporations represented. The owner of each mutual fund share in turn receives a prorated slice of the net income.

In the meantime, the fund managers, watching the market closely, buy and sell portfolio shares, hopefully realizing a net profit from these transactions. The fund may, in the course of a year, realize $5 million in capital gains. It passes this money along to its shareholders, too.

At the same time, however, the fund may be holding some stocks in its portfolio that have risen in value since the fund bought them. The fund may regard these shares as a good investment, likely to rise in value still further. Consequently, the fund may decide to hold them rather than sell. As these shares rise in value, the value of the over-all portfolio is increased, and with it the prorated value per share. This represents appreciation or unrealized capital gains as distinct from realized capital gains.

What this means is that the intelligent mutual fund shareholder watches three figures closely: (1) he watches the dividend payout he receives from the fund; (2) he watches the amount of capital gains distributed by the fund; and (3) he watches the net asset value of his shares.

(This last figure is printed daily in the financial section of many newspapers.) *These three figures tell him how well his investment is doing.*

Meanwhile, the fund is not only selling its own shares to the public; it is also redeeming shares turned back to it. Its ability to do so is maintained in two ways. First, most funds keep cash reserves to meet normal redemption requirements. Second, the inflow of money from the sale of new shares creates a pool of money out of which redemptions can be met.

The mutual fund system described here schematically has important tax characteristics as well. Thus, under the Internal Revenue Code, funds that meet certain requirements are permitted to distribute investment income and capital gains to their shareholders without first paying a tax on them. Most mutual funds take advantage of this provision. The fund is thus regarded, from a tax point of view, as a pipeline through which dividends, interest, and other income flow from the securities held in its portfolio to the mutual fund shareowner. Similarly, the fund serves as a conduit for capital gains. The individual mutual fund shareholder therefore treats investment income and capital gains received from his mutual fund exactly as he would treat them had he himself bought and sold securities without the mutual fund serving as an intermediary.

For tax purposes, the shareholder receives from the fund a year-end statement telling him clearly what part of the sums distributed to him represent dividends from the fund and what part represents long-term capital gains. He also receives from the fund regular statements that not only tell him how his own investment is faring but also report on the progress of the fund, detailing its portfolio holdings, its expenses, changes in management, and other relevant data. Before he buys, he receives a prospectus that carefully explains the objectives and operations of the particular fund.

Funds are not foolproof, and they take great pains to point this out to prospective shareholders. Under penalty of law, they must make full disclosure. A typical statement included in the prospectus of a fund recently read as follows: "While this prospectus points out certain advantages in owning shares . . . you should understand that the Fund cannot eliminate the risks inherent in investing in securities whose prices are subject to market fluctuations, and there can be no assurance that the objectives will be achieved."

After reading such cautionary messages, millions of investors continue to buy mutual fund shares, presumably because they have found that the money-making mechanism, by and large, seems to work well. The potential rewards clearly seem to them to outweigh the risks.

To sum up, then, a fund sells shares to the public. It invests the money it receives for these shares in the securities of other corporations. As these other corporations declare dividends, the fund collects them and, after paying expenses, passes them along to its own shareholders. When the fund sells some of its portfolio securities at a profit, it passes along this profit (minus whatever losses it may have sustained) to its shareholders in the form of a capital gains distribution—usually at the end of the year. As the value of the remaining securities in the portfolio rises or declines, the value of each individual mutual fund share rises or declines. Any time the mutual fund shareholder wishes to redeem his shares, the fund buys them back at the current net asset value.

This ingenious mechanism offers the mutual fund shareholder diversification, since the fund usually holds a portfolio that is much more diversified than any he himself could afford. It offers him the expert services of professional investment counselors who watch the markets closely on a full-time basis, often (as we shall see later) using elaborate research methods to determine which securities to buy or sell and the appropriate time to do so. Finally, the fund mechanism offers the shareholder high liquidity.

The fund mechanism, fortunately, can be tuned up, modified, or adjusted to serve many different purposes. Investors pursue a variety of objectives. So do mutual funds. To understand why they lend themselves to so heterogeneous a group of investors, it is essential to see how heterogeneous the funds are themselves. Like investors, they come in all sizes and shapes. It is the differences among funds that will occupy us next.

The Risk-Reward Spectrum

Chapter Four

Sɪɴᴄᴇ the needs of different investors vary, and the needs of the same investor vary from time to time, the mutual fund industry has developed a variety of fund types to meet different investor purposes. To have done otherwise would be, as one fund president put it, "like making uniforms for the U.S. Army to the measurement of the average man."

The individual who so desires can hire an investment counselor who, for several thousand dollars a year, will oversee the investor's portfolio. The counselor, if he is a good one, will not only alter the mix of the portfolio to correspond to market potentials but will also alter it to suit the distinctive requirements of the investor. In effect he designs a personalized investment policy for the client, then executes it for him.

This kind of service, which is sometimes regarded as the financial equivalent of a custom-made suit, is clearly too expensive for most Americans. Of course, while the $250 custom-made suit *may* outlast a $75 suit, price alone is no *guarantee* of a superior product. Moreover, many investment counselors will not touch an account under

$300,000, and many others who do take on small accounts guarantee only partial service. They are not being snobbish; they simply cannot afford to handle small accounts at the one-half of 1 per cent fee that is more or less standard for this service. At this rate, a $100,000 account brings in $500, which is like asking a man to supervise the investment of $1000 for a fee of $5. Individualized service is simply not feasible at that price.

It was this fact of life that gave birth to the mutual fund industry. The earliest funds actually were extensions of investment-counseling businesses. Typically, a counselor handling a number of large accounts would be asked by his clients to take on a small account for Aunt Margaret or Cousin John. Realizing the impossibility of servicing the small account profitably, some counselors hit upon the idea of pooling the small accounts, investing them in a single portfolio, and treating them as if they were a single large account, with the proceeds divided among the individual shareholders.

The portfolio would be invested in a wide diversification of stocks and bonds, to spread risk and to make it appealing to the largest number of potential investors.

Yet this innovation did not by itself overcome the problem of diversity. Some investors need and want a conservative portfolio; others require an adventurous list of securities. Some need immediate income; others want only long-term appreciation.

As the number of funds multiplied, they ranged themselves along what might be called a "risk-reward spectrum." At one end are solid, conservative, slow-moving funds. At the other lie funds that are more venturesome. The conservative ones usually offer somewhat higher dividends but more modest appreciation and lower risk. The more venturesome offer increased potential gain along with increased risk. Today the more than 375 funds in existence are finely graded from one end of this spectrum to the other, and a perceptive investor can usually find one precisely attuned to his individualized needs.

If one examines the funds that lie at either extreme of the spectrum, the differences among them will be sharp and easily identifiable. But since this spectrum is divided into more than 375 subdivisions, the differences between one fund and the adjacent one are sometimes indistinct. Matters of nuance and shading become important, and it becomes difficult to classify funds neatly or easily.

Nevertheless, even with all these qualifications, it remains useful to view mutual funds as falling into one or another of several loose classifications, according to what their avowed investment objective is.

There are really only three basic investment objectives: income, growth of capital, and conservation of principal. There are, however, infinite combinations of these objectives, with many investors striving for all three, but with varying degrees of emphasis on one or the other. A fund fits into one classification or another depending upon the relative emphasis it places on one or another of these objectives.

Funds may also be classified by the way in which they seek to attain these objectives. Here, too, there are three basically different types, with many subdivisions and shadings between them. The major types include:

1. *Bond-and-preferred-stock funds*. These funds sit at the most conservative end of the spectrum. They confine their investments to bonds, preferred stock, or both. Their objective is to provide stability and a relatively predict-

able amount of dividend income. Within this category there are variations according to the degree of emphasis placed on income and the degree of emphasis placed on stability.

Here is how one bond fund describes itself to prospective investors: "———— Fund has performed according to its investment objectives in providing relative stability of principal and reasonable return for the money entrusted to its care. . . . Stability has been an attainable objective. . . ." The fund's shares at the time of this report stood at close to a record high, but the fund took pains to point out that the value of its shares had not fluctuated "more than $1.00 per share over the past 20 years even though several severe changes in market prices occurred during this period." The same brochure announced the fund's seventy-sixth consecutive quarterly dividend.

For most investors, the bond fund's heavy accent on stability seems too conservative. There are today only a handful of bond-and-preferred funds, representing only a small percentage of the assets of the mutual fund industry. They are not intended to serve the broad mass of investors, and they do not.

2. *Balanced funds.* These funds invest in bonds, preferred stocks, *and* common stocks. Since bonds and preferreds are senior securities, less volatile than common stocks, they act as a built-in stabilizer in a fund. When signs seem to point toward a market downturn, the managers of a balanced fund as a rule sell common stock and increase their holding of bonds and preferreds. They reverse action when the market looks healthy and rising. By shifting the ratio of common stocks to bonds and preferreds in the portfolio, they attempt to achieve optimum results.

An example of how this works is cited by an official of one of the largest balanced funds in the country:

In 1956–1957 price/earnings ratios had gotten up well above 20 on the stocks in our portfolio—that is, the stocks were selling for 20 times their annual reported earnings. At the same time, bond market yields (interest rates) were going up and prices were going down. It just didn't seem sensible for us to have 73 per cent of our account in common stocks at high price/earnings ratios at a moment when things did not look too glowing anyway. And here were bonds, their prices going down and their yields going up, 4¼, 4½, on up to 5½ per cent. So between the end of 1956 and the fall of 1957 we sold some $24,000,000 worth of common stocks and moved more heavily into long-term bonds with interest rates running up as high as 5½ per cent. We cut our common stock position from 73 per cent to about 57 per cent. In late 1958 and 1959, when things looked better, we restored our equity position.

Then in the fall of '61 a little more froth came into the market. That was the time when growth stocks were very popular, and all the electronic stocks were coming out, and everything was coming out at seven and going to seventy. There wasn't anything particularly wrong with the economy. But there was all this frothy stuff—investment bankers coming out with 150,-000 shares of Gee Whiz Company, with aerospace contracts and that kind of thing.

So once more we began to prune back our common stock position. We sold between $13 and $16 million late in '61, before the '62 crash came along. I'm not trying to be immodest, but to illustrate how conservative management thinks about these things.

This kind of policy will not make the average investor rich overnight; but, done well, it will lead to appreciation of the net asset value of his shares along with a strong degree of safety.

The generally conservative line of balanced funds, less heavily committed to stability than bond funds but never-theless solid and prudent, has a broad appeal to the investing public.

3. *Common stock funds.* There are more funds in this category than in any other. Common stock funds or equity funds, as their names imply, tend to channel almost their entire investment into common stocks, giving up some of the stability offered by bonds and preferreds in return for better growth potential or current income. As a group, they tend to do well when the market as a whole does well and decline when the market declines. But even within this category there are substantial differences among funds.

For example, one leading common stock fund more or less limits its portfolio to what it calls "the royal blue chips"—General Motors, A.T. & T., General Electric and the like. This fund tells prospective shareholders that "over 95 per cent of the Fund's assets are in securities considered legal for purchase by savings banks in the State of New York. The other 5 per cent are in securities of insurance companies and of banks themselves." In short, within a framework of common stock investment, this fund has opted for the most conservative portfolio.

Others select their portfolio stocks for high current dividend output, for "future income," or for the likelihood of capital appreciation. There is considerable overlap among the objectives of common stock funds. They form the wide middle of the spectrum, and they account for a substantial part of all sales of mutual fund shares.

Within the common stock category are some funds that strongly emphasize capital appreciation and term them-selves "growth funds." In the words of one expert, "For growth funds it's not the income that counts, it's the out-come." Many lean toward what one fund has described as "companies with established and recognized growth char-acteristics such as sharply rising demand for their prod-ucts, modern technology, advanced marketing techniques, scientific orientation, or intensive research programs. They therefore offer above-average, long-term prospects for rising earnings and dividends."

Many growth funds include in their portfolio such solidly established companies as IBM, Columbia Broad-casting, Eastman Kodak, and even some fast-growing utility stocks. Other growth funds are more risk-oriented and eschew the large, established companies in favor of less-known corporations whose stock is selling at relatively low prices. One such fund notes that "the stocks of many leading corporations were at one time low-priced issues, and it is reasonable to assume that certain companies whose stocks are low in price today will prosper and grow into business leaders of tomorrow." In the portfolio of this fund one might find, for example, the Aztec Oil & Gas Co., Metromedia, Inc., Itek Corp., and Beech Aircraft Corp.

Still another variant of the growth fund might be called the "capital appreciation fund." While the traditional growth fund emphasizes long-term gains, the appreciation fund sometimes seeks out special situations, depressed industries about to recover, or "turnaround" companies. The distinction between this and the ordinary growth fund is that the appreciation fund places less emphasis on long-term investments.

Ranging funds on the risk-reward spectrum is only one possible way of categorizing them. Moreover, as sug-gested earlier, the categories are anything but air-tight;

and the more funds there are, the greater the likelihood of overlapping objectives among them. For the individual investor, it sometimes helps to think of them in terms of the degree to which they stress stability, immediate income, or growth and/or future income.

Whichever system is used, the fact remains that the basic mechanism of the mutual fund has now been adapted to serve the investment objectives of a very wide range of investors. In the process of expanding, the industry has also come up with a rich variety of systems under which individuals can invest, and an even richer variety of services and arrangements.

Chapter Five

A
Diversity
of
Uses

I<small>N</small> 1952 in Pasadena, California, the forty-seven-year-old proprietor of a dry cleaning store listened noncommittally to a mutual fund salesman. The man and his wife were childless. They worked together in their store and lived behind it. The salesman had arrived early for another appointment up the street. While waiting, he decided to try his luck with the cleaning-store people.

As a result of this and a second call on them, the couple opened two mutual fund accounts. They placed $3500 in a balanced fund and another $450 in a common stock fund. The money came from their account in a savings and loan association, but they had other cash savings so that they would not be hard-pressed for immediate financial needs. From then on the couple made monthly investments in the common stock fund—usually between $100 and $200, occasionally more, depending upon how well their business was doing. They also reinvested all the dividends they received from the fund.

In 1954 they sold their store for about $15,000 and put the full sum into their common stock fund. By then they had accumulated a total of about $27,000 in this fund.

In December, 1957 the couple decided to take it a bit easier and moved to Laguna Beach. They redeemed $5700 worth of shares to help purchase a new home, and they thereupon began to withdraw $250 a month from the fund for living expenses, supplementing income they were receiving from other sources.

In 1963, disenchanted with beach life, the couple decided to return to the city. They redeemed $30,000 worth of shares from the fund account (which, by now, despite withdrawals, had grown to $39,000). Using this, plus the money realized from the sale of their Laguna Beach home, they bought a small apartment house in town.

More recently, in February 1965, they withdrew another $12,000 from the fund to help purchase another piece of property. Altogether, over the years, this couple put a total of $24,714 into the common stock fund, including the value of reinvested dividends. As of April 1965, they had withdrawn close to $50,000, and still had $4500 in the fund. They also had the accumulated value of the money they had placed in the balanced fund.

This case history—in which names have been omitted and certain facts changed slightly to preserve the privacy of the couple—illustrates a fact about mutual funds that many investors overlook. According to *Management Investment Companies,* a study issued by the Commission on Money and Credit, "The postwar period has been marked by the development of many important service features by the investment companies."

What this means, simply put, is that a mutual fund investment now has a flexibility and versatility it lacked in the beginning. Not only may an investor choose among different funds; he may also choose a system of investment that suits his personal needs, and he may change his mind later on and adopt a different approach. The couple cited above is interesting because they made use of several of the service characteristics of a mutual fund investment.

The "classic" mutual fund investment is the *regular account* formed by an investor who makes a single purchase of a block of mutual fund shares with a lump sum of money. The money then stays in the fund under professional management until such time as the investor wishes to redeem his shares.

A simple variation of this is the dividend reinvestment account under which the fund, instead of paying dividends to the shareowner, automatically reinvests them in additional shares. The shareowner, of course, has the option of choosing between receiving his dividends or reinvesting them.

A further variation of the *regular account* is the *accumulation plan.* Different funds have different names for it, but it is nothing more than a program under which the investor adds to his investment at regular—usually monthly—intervals. This is what the dry cleaner did at the beginning. Ordinarily, the plan makes it possible for the investor also to reinvest his dividends and capital gains automatically.

Some accumulation plans are completely voluntary. The investor can skip months or drop the plan at any time. Others—often termed "contractual"—involve a formal agreement under which an investment program is spelled out, usually for ten or fifteen years. In these, the shareholder commits himself to regular investment. If he terminates the program during its early years, he pays an effective sales charge greater than that paid on a voluntary plan.

Regular investments have a way of adding up, and one fund likes to tell the story of the New York businessman who on May 5, 1949, opened an accumulation account by making an initial investment of $1000. Every month thereafter the businessman added $100. He also reinvested all his dividends and took his capital gains distributions in the form of additional shares rather than cash. By May 15, 1966, seventeen years after he started, the owner of this account, having invested $21,400 and reinvested his dividends, owned 16,310 shares of the fund with a value of $60,836.

One side advantage of an accumulation account is that it may result in dollar cost averaging, a system based on the investment of even dollar amounts at regular intervals, regardless of the then-current price of the shares. Through this method the investor receives more shares for the same number of dollars when the market price is low, and fewer shares when the net asset value is high. This reduces his risk: he loses the opportunity to buy all his shares at low price levels, but also avoids the possibility of buying them all at peak prices. If carried out consistently, dollar cost averaging also results in his purchase of shares at an average *cost* lower than the average of the prices at which the shares were purchased.*

Accumulation plans are gaining in popularity. Ten years ago there were fewer than 300,000 such plans on the books. At the end of 1966 there were about 2,900,000.

The opposite of the accumulation plan, also illustrated by the case of the Pasadena couple, is the *withdrawal account*. This also goes under a variety of names, depend-

* See foonote on page 40.

ing upon the fund, but the basic idea is simple. It amounts to a systematic redemption program. Withdrawals can be used to supplement living expenses, as in the case above, to support a dependent, to provide extra money during an illness, to meet mortgage payments, to pay educational expenses, or for any other purpose. (*The Wall Street Journal* reported the case of a man who used his withdrawal account to pay alimony to a former wife. The man's second wife became peeved, the paper reported, when she saw monthly alimony checks in the family checkbook records. The man soothed her ruffled feelings by setting up a withdrawal account and having the monthly withdrawals sent to his ex-wife.)

* Assume an investor purchased $100 worth of mutual fund shares on the first of each month for six months. Let us also assume the price of each share varied from month to month as indicated below:

	Price per share	Number of shares purchased by $100 investment
January	$20	5.0
February	18	5.5
March	16	6.2
April	20	5.0
May	22	4.5
June	24	4.2
Average Price	$20	Total Number Purchased 30.4

The investor would thus have invested a total of $600 and received 30.4 shares. This means that each share cost him an average of $19.73 ($600 ÷ 30.4 = $19.73), or 27 cents less per share than the average of their prices on the dates of purchase.

These figures, while not exact, illustrate the advantages of dollar cost averaging. It should be noted that the real value of this system manifests itself over a long period of time, not the relatively brief span of six months shown here.

The Wall Street Journal described withdrawal plans in these terms:

A minimum purchase of $10,000 of the fund's shares is required. (A few funds set a $5000 minimum.) These shares then are put in the custody of a bank, although the investor can discontinue the program and get his capital back any time he wants. The investor specifies the [monthly] amount of [money] he wants from his investment, and a check for the proper sum is automatically mailed to him. . . . If dividends on the shares aren't sufficient to meet the scheduled payments, some of the shares themselves are sold to make up the difference.

Thus, the investor risks depletion of his capital. . . . But there's also the chance that rising stock prices will more than offset any sales of shares, allowing the investor to get his regular [monthly check] and at the same time see the market value of his original investment grow. The investor is in effect betting on a bull stock market.

Still another service lies in the conversion privilege many funds make available. Companies that manage mutual funds often sponsor more than one. These funds are usually designed to meet differing investment objectives. A fund-sponsoring organization may offer the public shares of a balanced fund, a common stock fund, a growth fund, or any combination of these and other types. One organization distributes the shares of ten funds that range from bond-and-preferred all the way to ultragrowth. From time to time, the investment objectives of individual shareholders change. They may become more conservative or more aggressive. The conversion privilege makes it possible for an investor to switch from a fund with one objective to another with a different objective in the same group at a substantially lower rate of sales charge, or at nominal cost (usually $5 per transaction).

As the mutual fund industry has grown, it has developed additional features of interest to various investors. For example, there are so-called *exchange* funds which permit an investor to buy shares without putting up cash at all: he "exchanges" shares he may hold in various corporations for their equivalent in fund shares. Unlike ordinary funds, which accept additional investments from their shareholders at any time, the exchange fund is only open to investment during a specified period of time. After that the shareholder has the right to redeem at any time, but he may not buy additional shares.

The exchange fund arrangement has the effect of permitting an investor, with a sizable chunk of stock that has already appreciated sharply, to shift from a nondiversified to a diversified position without paying capital gains tax at the time of the exchange of his shares. However, a change in the tax laws at the end of 1966 probably means that no new exchange funds will be formed.

There are also arrangements under which a mutual fund investor can create a *trust* for any of a variety of purposes. An elderly man may use his shares to set up a trust that will give his wife income for life, with the remainder after her death going, for example, to a child or grandchild. In Los Angeles the widow of a prominent surgeon used $100,000 to open six different mutual fund accounts naming herself as trustee and setting up a different beneficiary for each trust. The large amount of the initial investment made it possible for her to buy the shares at a reduced commission. On her death, proceeds of the trusts will be turned over to the beneficiaries. There will be no court probate costs. And so long as she lives she can change beneficiaries, sell shares, add to, or do anything else she wishes with the account.

Still another arrangement under which mutual fund shares can now be bought is linked to life insurance. Several funds offer accumulation plans under which the investor agrees to put a given number of dollars into the account over a stipulated number of years. A small part of the money is applied to the purchase of insurance so that the amount of insurance coverage is always equal to the amount that remains to be invested, in effect, guaranteeing completion of the investment program and thereby offering protection as well as investment.

Virtually all mutual funds encourage *automatic reinvestment* of dividends and capital gains distributions, a feature also made use of by the couple mentioned in the case history. By the end of 1966, 56 per cent of all mutual fund investors were taking their investment-income dividends in the form of additional shares; fully 75 per cent were accepting shares in lieu of capital gains distributions.

Finally, mutual fund shares can also be used as *collateral* for a loan at many U.S. banks. Thus one mutual fund salesman, himself a shareholder, uses his fund shares as collateral for a bank loan when he wishes to buy a new car. He reasons that in the long run the increase in the value of his shares will more than compensate for the bank interest.

The features described here help make the mutual fund instrument versatile. The sophisticated investor studies the services offered by the fund of his choice and makes use of those that are most helpful in advancing him toward his investment objective. Making a mutual fund investment properly, therefore, involves a two-step decision: first, the selection of an appropriate fund from among the types described in Chapter Four; second, selection of the most appropriate plan or service features. All of this naturally raises the question of cost, one that leads to a consideration of the charges, fees, and commissions involved in mutual fund investment.

Chapter
Six

The
Cost
of
Services
Rendered

Few financial subjects have been more analyzed and less understood than mutual fund fees and commissions. Articles and books have been written, studies made, and speeches delivered on this topic, but a large part of the public unfortunately remains confused about how much it costs to participate in a mutual fund.

The problem is simpler than it may sometimes seem. Mutual funds are not for people who expect something for nothing. The funds provide a range of services for the investor. They distribute and redeem shares, conduct research, manage a portfolio—in short, they operate a business, and the people who organize and run them expect to be paid for their work.

The individual who purchases mutual fund shares is buying not merely a security but a continuing service. He buys into a relationship that will continue until he redeems his last share, and it costs money to provide that service. If he wants the advantages that the mutual fund

[45]

form of investment can bring, he must be prepared to pay for it.

To calculate the true price of mutual fund services, the investor must understand that there are three distinctly different categories of cost involved. First, there is what is known as a "management fee." Second, there are other operating or administrative expenses. Third, there generally is a sales charge or commission.

If the investor keeps these three types of charges distinguished from one another, he will have relatively little difficulty steering himself clear of possible confusion.

In an earlier chapter, reference was made to the investment counselors sometimes employed by investors to manage their private portfolios. The investment counselor is responsible for telling his client what stocks or bonds to buy or sell, and when to do so. Sometimes he actually places buy and sell orders on the client's behalf.

Mutual funds, having developed out of the investment-counseling business, operate in much the same way. They, too, are managed by a professional investment counselor—in this case a company or group, not merely an individual—and pay the counselor a fee for management of the portfolio. This investment counselor is called the "manager" or "adviser" of the fund; the fee paid the adviser is called the "management fee" or the "advisory fee" and is the first of the three cost items passed along by the fund to the shareholder.

The management fee traditionally has amounted to one-half of 1 per cent of average fund assets per year or less. In recent years many fund advisers have introduced a sliding scale that ranges downward as the assets of the fund increase. In 1966 the management fee cost the average mutual fund shareholder less than .4 of 1 per cent.

This fee structure has been questioned on occasion. It has been noted, for example, that some investment counselors charge a fraction of a per cent less for managing private portfolios than the traditional fund management fee. What is overlooked in such comparisons, however, is the great difference in the size of the accounts being managed. As of 1960, for example, the average non-mutual fund account managed by an investment counselor was approximately $795,000. Even if this counselor charged the low rate of .25 per cent per year, this would have added up to a charge of $1987.50 against the average account. If he charged the full .5 per cent, the fee would be nearly $4000 a year.

In contrast, fund men point out, the average mutual fund account that same year was $3500. Thus even at a full .5 per cent, the average shareholder would have wound up paying only $17.50 for the management of his money for a year, less than the cost of a subscription to *The Wall Street Journal*.

The size of the management fee is of vital consequence to investment counselors or fund advisers, since these tiny percentages add up to large sums of money. For most individual mutual fund shareholders, however, a reduction of the management fee would yield inconsequential savings.

In calculating the cost of any mutual fund investment, the shareholder should begin by figuring out the management fee that will be charged against him. He can look it up in the fund's prospectus.

The second element of cost a mutual fund shareholder bears comes under the general heading of *other operating expenses.* These cover the costs of custodian fees to banks, legal and auditing fees, printing expenses, state and local taxes, and so on. For a large group of funds these might average between two-tenths and three-tenths of 1 per cent per year.

The third cost element is the *sales charge* or commission. The price of almost any commercial product or service available to the public—whether a pack of cigarettes or a yacht—includes some selling cost. This is also true of most mutual fund shares, and among the three different cost elements a mutual fund investor must bear in mind, the sales charge is usually the most important, particularly over the short term. It differs from the management fee and operating expenses in that, while these are deducted from the income paid to the shareholder, the sales charge is deducted at the time of investment.

On small purchases, the typical sales charge runs from about 7.5 per cent to about 8.8 per cent. But there is considerable variation, and some funds charge no sales commission at all. The sales charge is set forth clearly in each fund's prospectus, as are all other significant charges.

Above a certain point, the larger the shareholder's purchase, the smaller the commission is likely to be. Most funds establish a breakpoint ($10,000 or $25,000, for example) above which a reduced commission is charged. Various other devices also are used to offer lower rates. Some funds, for example, reduce the over-all level of commissions by charging the investor a smaller rate as his total holding grows. Some offer a "letter of intent" arrangement. Under this, an investor may indicate in advance his intention to purchase, say, $25,000 worth of shares over a period of time. If he does, he is charged only at the rate that would be applied if he had made the purchase all at once.

In assessing the sales charge, it is also important to remember that most funds charge nothing for redeeming a holder's shares, which means that the commission usually represents the cost of both buying *and selling* mutual fund shares.

Finally, there is a key point frequently overlooked by unsophisticated investors: the likelihood, based on experience, that the investor's shares will rise in value over a period of time. This, after all, is the purpose and premise of most investments. Since the commission is based on the amount of money being invested rather than the amount taken out of the account, the percentage usually turns out to be smaller than it seems in terms of eventual share valuation.

Critics of mutual funds have asserted that sales commissions are too high. "Too high related to what?" one fund official asks. "A sales charge is too high or too low only in relation to what is received for it. For example, on December 31, 1956, anyone who bought $10,000 worth of shares in the fund we manage paid a sales charge of $800. The buyer said, in effect, I think you can do more with $9200 over the years than I can do with $10,000. Was the sales charge too high? Ten years later, on December 31, 1966, the market value of his investment, assuming the reinvestment of all dividends and distributions, was over $27,200. This is what he received for the sales charge he paid.

"He might have done better or worse on his own, but the X-ingredient which attracts investors to mutual funds is the degree of assurance a good fund gives him that his investment will be successful if anybody's is, coupled with

the likelihood that it will be more successful than most."
The mutual fund shareholder, in other words, is buying
an expert service and the improved probability of success
that comes with it.

People frequently ask: How do mutual fund commissions compare with the cost of buying and selling corporate shares directly? The Wiesenberger annual, *Investment Companies,* cautions: "The investor who tries to
compare the selling charge on mutual fund shares with
the charges incurred for direct purchase of stocks should
make certain he is taking into consideration all relevant
facts. New York Stock Exchange Commission rates—
approximately one per cent, on the average, on the purchase of a 'round lot' [usually 100 shares]—are only part
of the story.

"Commissions and taxes are applied to sales of ordinary
securities as well as to purchases—whereas the mutual
fund charge usually covers both purchase and sale. In
addition to the broker's commission on all transactions in
listed securities, there are extra taxes and premiums on
odd-lot purchases and sales [orders for less than 100
shares]."

The Monthly Investment Plan, set up by the New York
Stock Exchange itself as a kind of do-it-yourself accumulation plan for those who wish to invest small amounts in
stock directly, may involve charges of 6 per cent going in
and as much as 6 per cent going out, a rate considerably
higher than the cost of a mutual fund investment.

Any comparison of mutual fund sales charges with
stock exchange commissions is an apples-and-oranges
proposition at best, however. Thus, for example, while
mutual fund shareholders do not pay exchange commissions directly—they pay only the management fee, operat-

ing expenses, and sales charge—the mutual fund itself does pay exchange commissions in the course of buying or selling securities for its portfolio, and these costs may also be regarded as a cost to the shareholder.

Considerations such as these lead the Wiesenberger annual to the conclusion "To compare the cost of buying mutual fund shares with the commission costs of buying securities directly can be both fallacious and misleading. It is fallacious because the two things compared are totally dissimilar. It can be misleading unless all important factors are taken into consideration. Practically speaking, the ultimate difference in cost between buying mutual fund shares and making direct investments is likely for most people to be small."

The reason the two are so different, of course, is that in buying a share of an ordinary corporation the purchaser is buying a piece of equity. But in buying a mutual fund share, he is buying equity *plus* a service contract that guarantees him professional management of his money as well as quick and easy liquidity.

He is also buying diversification, something that cannot be bought cheaply on the stock market.

The average price of a stock on the New York Stock Exchange is about $48 per share. Mutual funds usually hold in their portfolios upward of 100 different stocks. Assuming the investor seeks diversification but is satisfied with spreading his money across only 20 securities, he would have to buy $96,000 worth of stock at one clip to take advantage of the round-lot rate (100 shares each of 20 stocks at an average price of $48). This is clearly beyond the means of most investors. And the attempt to buy diversification for small sums of money would force the investor into paying odd-lot commissions instead of round-lot.

Thus, if an investor tried to invest $2500 in a list of 20 securities, he would wind up paying, for purchase and sale, a 10.7 per cent commission to his broker, against an average 8.4 per cent commission on a mutual fund investment that apportions his money over a far wider range of stocks.

If he invests $5000 over 25 individual securities, the broker's commission drops to 7 per cent—slightly lower than the mutual fund rate—but he gets considerably less spread for his money in return.

In short, even if in certain circumstances the mutual fund buyer pays more in commissions than the direct investor does, he receives much wider diversification in return.

All these figures have been calculated on the basis of mutual funds that charge the median commission. Some funds, as this implies, charge slightly more, and some considerably less—down to and including no commission at all.

These last are the so-called *no-load* funds; they charge no sales commission because, in a certain sense, they do not *sell* shares. An investor who wants them must *buy* them—he must take the initiative and contact the fund directly. Such funds have no sales organization and their shares are usually not available through brokers. Some no-loads do charge a 1 per cent commission when the investor redeems his shares.

"How can no-load funds afford to operate without charging a sales commission?" is a frequent question. The answer is that their sponsors incur no sales expenses to speak of and make their money from the management fee alone. Other sponsors receive the management fee plus the commission, but the commission is often eaten up by the actual costs of selling. Few fund advisers make any significant money from the sales commission. Most of it is paid out to broker-dealers, salesmen, advertising agencies, and others. The management fee rather than the sales commission is the key to profitability for most mutual fund sponsors.

One last fact about sales commissions needs to be mentioned here: commissions on *contractual plans,* sometimes called "front-end loads."

The contractual plan, described in the preceding chapter, is an arrangement under which the investor makes monthly or quarterly payments into the fund for a stipulated period ranging up to ten years or more. In a voluntary accumulation plan the investor's commissions are spread evenly over all his purchases. In a contractual plan, the commissions are bunched heavily into the first year and sharply reduced in subsequent years, so that the investor who buys a contractual plan and discontinues it in the early years may find he has paid a higher rate of commission on the amount invested than if he had started a regular account or voluntary accumulation plan.*

* By law, commissions on a contractual plan may never exceed 9 per cent of the total dollars to be invested, and no more than half of any periodic investment during the first year may go for sales commissions.

In practice what happens is that on, say, a $6000 plan spread over a ten-year period, the shareholder would put in $50 per month. Since the full plan calls for payment of $6000, the top commission that can be charged would be 9 per cent of that amount, $540. Of this amount $300 would probably be deducted from the first year's payments (totaling $600). The remaining $240 of commissions would be deducted equally from the payments over the next nine years.

Depending upon the actual percentage charged (the above example

The front-end load has been criticized because of this fact. Sponsors of contractual plans point out that the system was originally adapted from practices in the life insurance industry, where a front-end load is standard and where the relative proportion of the first year's premium that goes to sales commissions is usually much heavier than the load on a mutual fund contractual plan. They argue that the existence of this feature serves as encouragement to investors to keep up their investment program. They adduce statistics that prove that contractual-plan holders tend to fulfill their programs much more frequently than voluntary plan holders, and that relatively few contractual plan investors actually drop out and suffer a cash loss.

Contractual plans are increasingly popular, especially among small investors. Many of these make investments so small (as little as $10 a month) that without the front-end load there would be insufficient incentive for a salesman to call on them. They are, in effect, buying a service that will discipline them to invest. According to contractual plan sponsors, if investors fulfill their program, they will have paid little, if any, more than a voluntary-plan holder and may have a backlog of assets they would otherwise probably never have built up.

In summary, the investor interested in a mutual fund investment must weigh the cost of the *management fee*, the

---

was premised on the maximum 9 per cent), as well as on the size of the investment and the duration of the plan, monthly commissions after the first year may drop down as low as 1 per cent. Generally, charges are lower on voluntary plans up to the level of $200 or $250 a month. Above that, the contractual plan may turn out to be less expensive. But since more money is taken out early, less goes to work for the investor at the very start, and there may be some additional loss of advantage even at the higher level of payments.

operating expenses, and the *sales commission* against the value of services performed for him. *The management fee and operating expenses combined usually add up to considerably less than 1 per cent annually. The sales commission, which is charged by most though not all funds, may range up to 8 or 9 per cent.*

What must be remembered is that whatever the total cost, it will be worth it if the performance of the fund justifies it. If, however, over the long term the fund fails to perform, if the investment mechanism breaks down, even microscopic charges may not be worth it. Cost is relevant only when measured against results; it is performance that counts.

Purpose and Performance

Chapter Seven

In March 1933 Franklin Delano Roosevelt became President of the United States. Two days later a financial crisis forced the closing of American banks. As the new President took firm hold, a brief wave of optimism strengthened the economy of the country. Between then and July, Wall Street experienced an upsurge. Industrial stock prices rose sharply. Monthly volume shot up from less than 20 million shares in January and February to 125 million in June. Then on July 21 the market crashed once more. Echoes of 1929 reverberated through the canyons of Wall Street. The country was gripped by a wave of strikes. Farmers were in turmoil as farm prices thudded. Several long years of depression still lay ahead of the American people.

Nevertheless, had some brave investor on December 31 of that bleak year taken $10,000, bought the shares of at least one actual mutual fund, and subsequently reinvested his dividends and capital-gain distributions, he could have sat back and received $32,736 on the same date ten years later. Had he left his money in and continued to invest dividends and capital gains, by 1966 his original investment would have grown to over $600,000.

In fact, a ten-year investment in this fund beginning on

any date from 1933 to 1956 would have made money for him. The best time would have been December 31, 1949. A ten-year investment beginning then would have increased to $45,939. On the average, counting reinvested dividends as part of the cost, an investment would almost exactly have doubled in a ten-year period.

No investor who put his money into this fund and left it there for a full decade would have lost a penny, despite years of crisis—war, boom, or bust. Nor was this fund unique. Indeed, the striking fact about mutual funds in general is that, during the last thirty years, a shareholder who invested in virtually any mutual fund and left his money in it over a long enough period of time was likely to make money. This cannot be said of many who invested directly in corporate stocks without using a fund as an intermediary. Virtually any broker's list of clients would be bound to include some who have lost money despite the duration of their investment.

This is why one mutual fund executive claims that "for an investor wishing to share in the growth of the American economy, a mutual fund offers the highest degree of probability of any investment. The truth of this statement has been borne out time and again."

It is necessary, however, to underscore the importance of time. According to Jordan and Dougall's *Investments,* a leading textbook on finance, "Performance over short periods is not representative, and the average annual performance over a period may have been affected by one or two especially good or bad years. It is the year by year and cumulative records that are important." So long as the general direction of the American economy is upward, time is on the side of the investor.

Do mutual fund shareholders really hold onto their

shares long enough to reap their advantage? According to a survey quoted in *Private Financial Institutions,* a study issued by the Commission on Money and Credit, "for those shareholders of investment companies ten years ago, 72 per cent still own their shares, but 28 per cent have redeemed them. Moreover, of these 72 per cent of shareholders ten years ago, one half or 36 per cent have been holders for 15 years or more." Shareholders seem fully aware that mutual funds should be viewed as long, rather than short-term, investments.

Nor should it be assumed that the 28 per cent who redeemed their shares lost money. A good number of those made money, but redeemed because of a change of investment objective or because they needed money for some other purpose. One survey has revealed that of a group of 3400 mutual fund shareholders who redeemed their holdings, 83 per cent reported a net gain when they cashed in. Four per cent broke even. Only 13 per cent experienced a loss. It can be presumed with some certainty that the losers tended to be short-term investors.

Asked to judge the results, only 6 per cent of the redeemers felt that performance had been "poor." The remaining 94 per cent termed performance "excellent," "good," or "fair." This suggests that even among those who lost money, a sizable percentage, perhaps more than half, considered the performance of the fund, under the circumstances, to have been "fair" or better.

The mutual fund is not as a rule a medium for the maximization of profit, and most shareholders seem to know this, too. The fund provides a service, which might be defined as the prudent management of the investor's money in line with its announced objective. It is not out to make a killing for him; it *is* out to do a reasonably good job of caring for his money. As one top mutual fund official put it: "We're not trying to make people rich. We're trying to make them comfortable." A mutual fund should therefore not be expected to milk the last possible mill of profit out of an investment.

With this understood, investors who wish to rate funds with any degree of scientific precision must take into account several factors. The first has to do with investment objective.

Some mutual fund men draw a little diagram to illustrate this point:

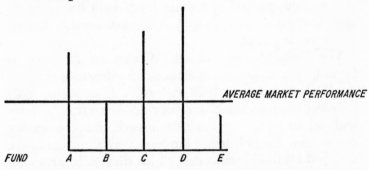

They ask the customer to guess which fund performed best and which worst. Most investors need only a glance to point to Fund D as the best performer and Fund E as the worst.

Yet, as fund executives explain, quite the reverse may be true; it is impossible to measure a fund in the abstract. The performance of a fund can only be measured in relation to its objective.

It is true that Fund D performed at a rate that far exceeded the market as a whole. Yet if Fund D were a bond-and-preferred fund with a primary objective of stability and preservation of capital, the performance shown on the diagram would indicate that the fund probably took undue risks. Reward in the market is usually in direct ratio to risk, and bond funds are not supposed to play games. Consequently, if Fund D were a bond fund, what seemed to be good performance may in fact have been bad. On the other hand, if Fund E were also a bond fund, what appeared to be bad performance may have been exactly right. A Mariner rocket may shoot 100 million miles into space, but if it is not heading toward Mars, it is off course and its performance is inappropriate.

With these considerations in mind, it becomes clear that *any comparison of mutual funds with market averages is fraught with danger.* A market average has no objective. It just *is.*

The University of Chicago's Center for Research in Security Prices, for example, made an exhaustive study of stock prices between 1926 and 1960. It examined 1700 different common stocks and concluded that if an investor had put an equal investment into each company having one or more issues listed in the New York Stock Exchange and had faithfully reinvested all his dividends, he would have received over the entire thirty-five-year period a return equal to 9.01 per cent compounded annually. During some time periods the return would have been even better. In the decade 1950–1960, for example, the return would have been 14.84 per cent.

The trouble with this kind of proposition is very simple. Few, if any, investors are in a position to buy stock in every company listed on the New York Stock Exchange. Similarly, the Wharton Report, a study prepared by a team of professors from the University of Pennsylvania, devoted a great deal of space to a detailed analysis of fund performance relative to the performance of Standard and Poor's 500 Stock Index. The Report found that an investor who bought shares of a mythical mutual fund that was the average of the 152 different funds studied would have doubled his money—increased his holding by virtually 100 per cent—within a 5¾-year period, assuming he reinvested all dividends and capital-gains distributions. Most investors, it is safe to assume, would have thought this growth reasonably good.

But the authors of the Wharton study pointed out that Standard and Poor's 500 Stock Index rose by 139.5 per cent in the same period. Why the difference?

First, among the 152 funds were a number of balanced funds and bond funds. The portfolios of these investment companies include bonds and preferred stock that, almost by definition, are less volatile than common stocks, whereas the index is based solely on common stocks.

Another point that had to be taken into account is the fact that funds offer their shareholders immediate liquidity. For this purpose they maintain part of their money in cash or short-term bonds in order to meet redemption demands as they arise. Consequently, not every dollar in the funds is working at full capacity in the market place; some are doing duty as guardians of the funds' liquidity.

When these factors are compensated for, it turns out that, dollar for dollar, the mythical average fund performed almost exactly as the S&P Index did. But the mutual fund figure, like the S&P Index, was nothing more than a metaphysical construct.

If the Index did as well as the average of 152 funds, why cannot an investor simply buy the stocks represented in the index instead of a mutual fund? There are very good reasons why he cannot. The difficulties of trying to meas-

ure fund performance by comparing it with market in-
dexes were dramatized in an internal memo prepared by
the head of an important Midwestern fund. Because so
many investors are tempted to make this kind of comparison, it is worth quoting from the memo at some length:

> The myth prevails that it would be simplicity itself to dupli-
> cate the performance of a stock market index such as the
> Dow-Jones Industrial Stock Average. . . . This myth is naïve;
> it disregards the difference between theory and reality. The
> Dow-Jones Industrials, and other well-known averages, are
> mathematical devices designed to show the approximate gen-
> eral trend of stock prices. As such, they enjoy a protected
> status, free of those complications of real investment life, such
> as brokerage commissions, odd lot differentials, taxes, fees,
> fractional shares, difficulties of execution of orders, ready
> availability of new money, etc.
>
> In fact, the one practically foolproof way of starting out
> worse than the Dow-Jones Industrials, and then . . . progres-
> sively doing worse than the Dow-Jones Industrials, is to buy
> the 30 stocks which on any given date make up that average.

The memo goes on to show how each time any of the
stocks in the average split, the investor would have the
problem of spreading the money represented by the additional shares he received over the entire list of thirty
stocks in proportion to their respective prices per share.
This is no problem for the armchair theoretician, but it is
incredibly difficult for an investor. In the words of the
memo:

"What is very simple in the mathematical formula for
computing the theoretical average is very complicated,
and very costly, and even impossible, in a living, breath-
ing, genuine investment portfolio."

For example, $2323.50 would have bought one share

each of the thirty stocks represented in the Dow-Jones Industrial Index at the close of business on June 17, 1964, just before a split in Woolworth stock. This split would have given the investor $56.17 to divide proportionately into thirty different stocks. Apart from the high odd-lot commissions he would face, he simply would not have been able to buy the fractional shares necessary. Five days later a split in A.T. & T. would have confronted him with the same problem again—the need to spread $69.37 over the thirty stocks. The result is that he would quickly find himself with part of his money in cash rather than stocks—and with a big broker's commission to boot.

To escape the problem of fractional shares, the investor would have had to place $95,263.50 into the thirty stocks —the smallest sum that would have given him enough of an investment to be able to spread the proceeds of the Woolworth split across the thirty stocks in full rather than fractional shares.

Even when the total amounts invested climb above the billion-dollar mark, the complications and costs are formidable. The Index itself keeps changing. In ten years there have been thirty-four changes in the Dow-Jones average arising out of splits, large stock dividends, rights, actual changes of the stocks in the Dow-Jones list, and so forth.

When all this is transferred to Standard and Poor's Index of 500 stocks, the complications escalate accordingly, until they become simply impossible to surmount. "The costs and handicaps of practical investing," the memo declares, "as compared with the cost-free simplicity of calculation of a market average, make it clear that the surest way to do worse than a market average, year after year, consistently and continuously worse, is to buy the stocks in that average."

What all this means is that *mutual funds, if they do no better than the market averages, may in practical dollar terms be outstripping them*. Many funds outpace the averages with regularity.

Leaving aside the academic question of buying the averages, a survey prepared by the economics staff of a leading Boston fund has revealed that *on December 31, 1950, if an investor had owned an equal position in each of fifty-one common stock mutual funds, so that he had a total of $10,000 invested, his holdings at the end of a ten-year period would have grown to $39,195, assuming reinvestment of all dividends and capital gains distributions. This, the report went on to say, "is the equivalent of a 14.63 per cent annual average rate of return."*

Is this a reasonable return? There can be no exact or universally acceptable answer. However, one relevant opinion is that of Winthrop Knowlton, now Assistant Secretary of the Treasury for International Affairs. In his book *Growth Opportunities in Common Stocks,* Mr. Knowlton says: "I believe that if you make an 8 per cent return on your common stock investments over a period of years, you can regard yourself as having earned a fair and satisfactory return. If you earn 10 to 15 per cent, you can be proud of yourself."

Certainly a return of 14.63 per cent would seem to fall within the definition of a mutual fund's purpose, "not trying to make people rich" but rather trying "to make them comfortable."

If the performance of mutual funds is to be measured against anything other than their own objectives, it should be measured not against mythical devices such as market averages or against random selections from the stock market, but against the performance of alternative investment media available to most investors in real life.

Oddly enough, while many attempts have been made to compare mutual fund performance with averages, no published report apparently exists of an attempt to analyze the record of individual investor accounts held by brokers for investors who purchase and sell corporate securities directly. Were one to go to any major brokerage firm and examine individual investor accounts over a period of time, he might come up with a worthwhile comparison of the difference between "doing it yourself" in the market place and hiring professionals to manage your portfolio.

Not only has no such study been made; one could not, in all likelihood, be made, for such information is a closely guarded secret. The same is generally true of results achieved by pension fund managers, individual investment counselors, bank-managed trust or agency accounts, or the investment managers of foundations and other institutions. In contrast, the performance of mutual funds is documented on a daily basis. Net asset figures for most funds are printed every day in many newspapers. Funds issue periodic reports to their shareholders. At least twice a year the shareholder receives a detailed description of the portfolio held by the fund. It is possible to find out in detail exactly what each fund is doing and what stocks it has sold and bought—in brief, it is possible to observe the professional money managers at work in mutual funds. But no similar data exist to make possible a comparison with alternative investment media.

It can be hoped that in the years to come data will be developed showing the relative performance of alterna-

tive investment media. Until this happens, most mutual
fund shareholders and the mutual funds themselves rely
on a different kind of comparison—a comparison of one
fund or class of funds with another of similar character.
Here, for example, is the way the president of a $1-billion
common stock fund describes the process of performance
evaluation followed in his company:

What we do here is to take ten or a dozen funds which we
know to have investment objectives similar to our own. We
can tell from our knowledge of their portfolio the amount of
risk they are willing to assume for their shareholders. Since
we are a large fund, we'll stick pretty much to other large ones,
the better-run, professionally run organizations. Then we keep
a constant watch—literally, daily, weekly, monthly, quarterly,
yearly comparisons of our performance in terms of income and
capital appreciation as against the others in the group.

Our objective then is to make sure we hold steady at a performance above the average for the group. If we do this, we
consider that we are performing satisfactorily.

A member of the board of another common stock fund
says: "If you find out of ten common stock funds your
company has fairly consistently been one of the poorer,
you begin to wonder. On the other hand, if you can find
one fund that is consistently in the upper half for its class,
that's a good way of testing."

Nor does one need to be an insider to make the same
kind of comparison. The mutual fund industry has grown
so large that a number of periodicals now do little else
than rank the funds one against the other. Perhaps the
most influential of these is the Wiesenberger annual, *Investment Companies. Johnson's Charts*, issued by Hugh
Johnson & Co., Inc., is another annual summary. The
Mutual Fund Directory of the *Investment Dealer's Digest*

does not directly compare funds, but presents year-by-year data from which comparisons can be made. The magazine *FundScope* provides monthly data on fund performance. *Barron's, Trusts and Estates, Forbes* and many other publications also report on the fund industry.

Each publication has its own system of classing and ranking the funds. The basic point is that, as noted earlier, there are three figures to watch. This is the key to measuring fund performance.

The first figure to watch is *income*, dividends and interest collected by the fund and passed along to its shareholders.

The second is *capital gains* distributions. This represents profits realized by the fund through the sale of portfolio securities previously purchased at lower prices.

The final figure is the net asset *value of the mutual fund share itself*. An increase in the net asset value reflects unrealized profits on its portfolio holdings (profits, in other words) that the fund could realize if it decided to sell rather than hold its portfolio.

How do we gauge performance? The simplest indication of performance, of course, is the fund's aggregate gain (a combination of all three figures). For example, here is a typical listing in the *Mutual Fund Directory*:

Statistical Record

Dec. 31	NAV*	Income	Capital Gains
1963	15.25	0.42	0.31
1964	17.04	0.45	0.18

* Net Asset Value

(Ordinarily, figures are shown for a full ten-year period.) What this table shows is that between the end of 1963 and the end of 1964 the fund in question distributed 45¢ per share in income derived from dividends and interest. It similarly doled out 18¢ per share in capital gains. The value of the share, reflecting unrealized capital gains, rose by $1.79. All three taken together add up to $2.42. If calculated against the value of the share—$15.25 on December 31, 1963—this works out to an over-all increase of roughly 16 per cent in one year.

By federal regulation, funds may never show their performance in such simple aggregate terms. They must make a clear distinction for the investor between income and capital gains, and they do. This system, however, can give the investor a quick rule-of-thumb indication of how his investment is faring.

Each of the fund-rating publications uses a somewhat different approach, which is why the various rating systems do not always show the same funds leading. The intelligent investor, however, can use the ranking system that most nearly reflects his own investment policy.

Most fund men caution that the rankings should not be taken literally. No fund can guarantee success. Even a twenty-five-year record of high performance would not (and cannot) of itself guarantee the investor that future performance will be as good. As in politics and in life generally, the historical record alone is not a sufficient basis for predictions of future action. Fund performance fluctuates. The intelligent investor will seek a fund in the right category that consistently does reasonably well, then not concern himself with whether or not some other fund is beating it this year.

The key thing is not that some fund whipped another in the ratings race or that it beat or did not beat the averages. In mutual fund performance, something else counts.

This was the point *Fortune* made when it summed up the issue: "When all is said and done, investors have flocked to mutual funds in recent years *not* because the funds are world-beaters every year, but because private investors would do less well on their own. . . . On the strength of their record, the mutual funds are an extraordinary success story, their success is merited and probably will go much further. They have opened up new doors for investors, great and small."

We have seen that a mutual fund is designed to provide diversification, liquidity, and professional management for investors. We have seen how funds pursue different objectives and we have canvassed the particular services they offer to their shareholders. We have also tallied up the cost of these services and examined the question of how to assess the performance of a mutual fund. What we have not yet seen is how the professional money managers work. We have yet to go behind the scenes in a mutual fund sponsor firm to see how research, careful decision-making, and skillful buying and selling make and remake a mutual fund's portfolio. In the three chapters that follow we shall do just this.

Part Two

THE
MONEY
MANAGERS
AT
WORK

The
Chapter # Rational
Eight # Investment

O~N~ a sunny afternoon in June 1965, a
group of mutual fund executives gathered around a table
at 61 Broadway to discuss industry matters. The market
had plunged and reared erratically for several days. No
one knew whether the worst was over or whether there
was more wild fluctuation to come. One of the executives,
a tall, slender, bespectacled man whose company manages
several fund portfolios, left the meeting for a minute to
look at a ticker in another room. When he came back he
announced that the market was still uneasy. So was he. As
he said to his colleagues, "This break has cut our asset
value by a hundred million dollars in the last few weeks."

The aggregate market value of the shares of the several
funds managed by his company had declined from $1.2
billion to $1.1 billion. Before many more weeks passed the
market had climbed again; his funds' shares were back at
the level they had been at before the flurry and were
climbing happily again. But the story gives some notion of
the size of the responsibilities borne by mutual fund managers. For this man and his company, a rise or dip of 8
per cent in stock prices can effect a $100-million change
in assets.

Managing the $35 billion invested in mutual funds is

not a job for amateurs. At least, that is the assumption of the 3,940,000 investors who turn their money over to the funds. The opposite of amateur management is professional management. But what exactly is professional management? How do the funds manage these billions?

The best way to find out is to look at a fund in action and listen to the money managers talk shop. Funds differ in detail from one another. They vary in tone, texture, and temperament. It is impossible to describe them all or to explain all the minute differences among them. It will therefore be useful to create a composite, a fictional fund that will serve to illustrate how most funds—give or take organizational and procedural variations—operate. For this reason, let us set up the Enterprise Management Company (EMC), an advisory organization responsible for managing the affairs of the Enterprise Balanced Fund, the Enterprise Common Stock Fund, and the Enterprise Growth Fund. In the chapters that follow we shall examine the workings of this mythical fund group. While the names of funds and individuals are fictional, the methods described are those widely used in the industry, and quotations are closely based on interviews conducted with real people working at real jobs in leading mutual funds.

EMC was formed in 1919 by Malcolm Osborne. The late Mr. Osborne was a broker for a time, then became a counselor to a number of large individual investors. In the early 1930's he took on a number of small accounts and pooled them into what subsequently became the Enterprise Balanced Fund. Later he started the two other funds. EMC is now presided over by his successor, Wilson Harris, a man in his early fifties.

The company, which today employs some sixty people,

The Rational Investment [75]

still serves as investment counselor to individuals and foundations. But it also sells its services to the three funds, which by now represent by far its most important source of revenue. For EMC did not create the three funds as a public service; in sparking them, it created customers for its own services. Today each of the funds pays EMC an annual management fee of .4 per cent to .5 per cent of the total assets held by the fund. Since the balanced fund has assets of $150 million, the common stock fund $100 million, and the growth fund $75 million, EMC is responsible for managing a total of $325 million in mutual fund money. It does this on behalf of 70,000 shareholders. It receives about $1.5 million as a management fee for its services. Indeed, these services are so substantial that it isn't necessary for the funds themselves to have employees of their own.

"The funds exist as a powerful legal entity," James D. Clarke, executive vice-president of the company, explains. "Each is, legally speaking, a corporation. But the funds didn't form themselves. The management company has spent years and a lot of money creating them. It takes money to get a fund off the ground. Even after they are started, it's a long time before they amount to anything in the way of income for the sponsor. A ten-million-dollar fund, for example, would pay the sponsor only fifty thousand dollars a year, so you can imagine the terrific time and expense that the sponsoring company absorbs in the early years. Fifty thousand dollars doesn't begin to pay for what it costs to manage a mutual fund."

EMC, therefore, having created the Enterprise funds, then stands, essentially, in the position of a contractor supplying advisory and management services to them.

Critics of mutual funds sometimes object to this relationship on grounds that it is not completely at "arm's length." According to this line of reasoning, the funds should shop around for investment advice rather than allow themselves to be linked organically to a single adviser. In this way, wide-open competition could prevail and the funds could presumably get the best advice available.

At the same time, these critics hold, there is a conflict of interest between the management firm or adviser (which wants to charge the largest possible management fee) and the fund, which ought to pay the smallest possible fee.

These arguments overlook the essential historical fact that the funds simply would not exist had not the management companies created them at considerable risk and expense to themselves. As an official of one leading fund wrote to a shareholder: "It is the manager-sponsor firm that creates the fund, undertakes to provide all the services of investment management and administration, distributes the fund's shares, spends money on promotion and advertising, and, in short, makes the fund grow and be successful. When the fund is small, these activities are a losing proposition for the manager-sponsor. If the fund grows to a substantial size, however, these activities can be carried on at a profit. This is the essence of our business."

As to the supposed conflict of interest between the adviser firm and the shareholders, the possibility of such a conflict was taken into consideration by those who originally wrote the federal legislation governing mutual fund operations. Certain safeguards for the share holder thus are built into the legislation.

Each of the funds managed by EMC, for example, is headed by its own board of directors. This board consists in part of EMC officers, but also includes directors who are not affiliated in any way with EMC. These are prominent businessmen, retired military officers, lawyers, several educators and one scientist.

These independent directors have specific responsibilities. The Investment Company Act of 1940, for instance, requires that the renewal of a contract between a fund and its advisory firm must be approved each year, either by vote of the shareholders or by a majority of non-affiliated directors.

According to Jim Clarke, "No fair-minded person can question that if a fund's performance is consistently poor, relative to other comparable funds, it is the duty of the directors to do something about it." In fact, directors can and do suggest improvements in the investment adviser's services and see that these are carried out.

Professional management as the term is used at EMC, Clarke explains, means that, under the supervision of the funds' boards of directors, the sponsor must not only manage and invest the funds' portfolios, but must also handle all their administrative work for them and distribute their shares. *Invest. Administer. Sell.* These three functions determine the internal organization of Enterprise Management Company. Thus there is an Investment Division, an Administrative Division, and a wholly owned subsidiary, Enterprise Fund Distributors, Inc., that carries out the sales function.

The table of organization of the company looks something like this:

ENTERPRISE MANAGEMENT COMPANY, INC.

*WILSON HARRIS, PRES.

*JAMES D. CLARKE, EXEC. V. P.

INVESTMENT DIVISION	ADMINISTRATIVE DIVISION	ENTERPRISE FUND DISTRIBUTORS, INC.
*HAMILTON KRAMER, V.P.	JOHN LINGLE, V.P.	HARRY WRIGHT, PRES.

RESEARCH DEPARTMENT	PORTFOLIO DEPARTMENT	
*JOSEPH MITCHELL, DIR.	*JAMES WILLIAMSON, PORTFOLIO SUPERVISOR	
ECONOMIC ANALYSIS	BALANCED FUND	
TECHNICAL ANALYSIS	COMMON FUND	
FINANCIAL ANALYSIS	GROWTH FUND	
STATISTICAL SERVICES	TRADING ROOM	

*INVESTMENT POLICY COMMITTEE: HARRIS CLARKE KRAMER MITCHELL WILLIAMSON

Before going on to see how the other major functions are performed, it will be helpful to examine the investment operation—the heart of the company—to see how $325 million is invested, how decisions are made to buy or sell portfolio securities, and how those decisions are carried out. A good place to begin is the Research Department.

As EMC's Director of Research Joseph Mitchell explains: "A rational investment policy must be based on knowledge, and we believe that the value of any security is affected by three factors. First, the company. Second, the stock market. Third, the economy and the world situation generally.

"While just about all the major mutual fund managers employ a staff of securities analysts," he says, "some do not have a staff economist. Some don't do much technical analysis of the market. We believe we ought to do research on all three levels. I'm not saying ours is the only way to do it. This just happens to be our approach, and obviously we think we're right."

The company economist, in turn, explains his function this way: "Investment decisions shouldn't be made in a vacuum. The strength of any company and the condition of the market are both influenced by broad economic factors. It's my job to keep up with these." He points to a pile of papers at one end of his desk and begins to peel things off the top of the pile. The first item is entitled the *Federal Reserve Bulletin.* Next is the *Survey of Current Business* of the Department of Commerce, followed by a mimeographed study of capital goods production, reports of the Tax Foundation, a report on government health programs, and a speech by an official of the Deutsche Bank in which the speaker discussed the German attitude toward the U.S. balance-of-payments problem.

"There's a constant flow of this stuff," the economist says, shuffling the pages, "along with material put out by various brokerage houses and an endless stream of government data. I spend most of my time examining this material, reporting on it, filtering it, analyzing it from the point of view of its possible effect on profits. I also go down to Washington now and then to see people at the Budget Bureau, the Treasury Department, or the Federal

Reserve Board. And I attend the important economic conferences."

The result of all this is a series of economic intelligence reports prepared by the economist and his assistant. In recent months he has put together special reports on the impact of ocean-freight rates on the balance-of-payments problem; the implications of population trends for the teen-age market; and the outlook for profits in the manufacturing industries. In addition, there are periodic reports on the general state of the economy.

"We try," he says, "to come up with an integrated picture of the over-all economic condition and climate; this is distributed to all our people here. This broad picture helps them put in perspective the detailed information they collect about specific industries or companies."

The work of the economist is supplemented by the fund's "market analysis" staff. Their base is a room, the walls of which are lined with charts and graphs on which are plotted interest rates, a ranking of industry groups according to investor preference, and a series showing the day-to day performance of the Enterprise funds. In cabinets lining the walls are hundreds of other charts and graphs, assiduously kept up to date by a small staff.

The technical analysis staff measures buying and selling pressures behind the price movements of individual stocks and the groups to which they belong. It also studies the shifts in investor sentiment among various types of common stocks—stable, cyclical, or growth—and relates these shifts to over-all market conditions. It continually evaluates the price potentials of individual stocks from a technical point of view and prepares periodic reports on the state of financial markets. These are channeled, like the economist's reports, through the research chief to all members of the research department.

Immediately down the corridor from this room is still another small office, this one occupied by the head of statistical services. His job is to provide the economist, the technical analysis staff, and—most important—the financial analysts, with a continuing flow of data churned out by a computer in the basement of the building.

According to the chief statistician, EMC "keeps tabs on twelve hundred different securities by computer—their price, their earnings for the last four years, and estimated earnings for the next year. This is kept up to date daily and given to our research people every morning along with a complete list of the securities in our fund portfolios.

"Since each of our funds has a different objective, we analyze all securities of companies over a certain size and eliminate those that seem totally inappropriate at the moment for any of the three funds. We then come up with a group or 'panel' of stocks suitable to each fund. Portfolio selections are made from these panels.

"The computer makes it possible for us to maintain performance and estimated earnings records for each of the stocks on the panels. It compares the performance of each stock with the Dow-Jones 'average, Standard and Poor's Index, with other stocks in the same industry and the others in the same panel. It tells us how the panel is performing against the market in general and whether any particular stocks ought to be dropped or added to the panel. We're still at the beginning of computer analysis. But the industry is learning more and more about it as time goes by."

It would be a mistake, however, to leave the impression

that a stock is picked for an Enterprise fund portfolio by computer, he adds hastily. "The computer output is evaluated in terms of what the economist has to say and what the financial analysts know about each individual company. The financial analysts, in fact, are the real key to the entire research operation. Many of the computer inputs are based on the judgment of the analysts. One of the advantages of this approach is that it forces our analysts to quantify their judgments. It sharpens their thinking."

Farther down the hall, a visitor is likely to meet a young man in shirtsleeves who turns out to be Francis Stephens, thirty-two, a graduate in economics from New York University's Graduate School of Business Administration. He has worked for EMC for five years. He is one of nine financial analysts employed by the company, each of whom is assisted by a secretary-statistician. Each analyst earns from $10,000 to $27,000 per year.

Financial analysts are assigned to cover one or more major industries. At EMC, for example, one man does nothing but watch the oil industry. Another covers utilities. Still another reports on electronics, electrical equipment, and data processing. Another covers chemicals and drugs.

Francis Stephens, assigned the chemical and drug group, explains his function: "My job starts when I get on the train in the morning. I read *The New York Times* on the way in. I might be interested in the implications of Medicare on the drug industry or something like that. In the office, I scan *The Wall Street Journal, Barron's,* and other financial journals—and, of course, the trade journals in my field of interest: *Chemical Week,* for example. Then there are brokerage houses that specialize in buying and selling for institutions like pension funds and mutual funds. They issue special reports on various companies and industries. These aren't like the short reports brokerage houses send out to the public. Since these are for institutional clients, they tend to be much fuller and more detailed.

"Our company retains several outside consultants. We go to them with special questions that might arise in our work—problems. We also retain as a consultant a former executive vice-president of one of the major chemical companies. He's recently retired, but he knows more about the industry than almost anybody. He channels information to us. A lot of my time is spent reading all this material and keeping in contact by phone and in person with these people. But about a third of my time is actually spent out on the road, meeting corporate officials and questioning them.

"Last Friday, for example, I got back from a two-day trip to Chicago, where I visited four companies. On Wednesday I met with Mr. Woodner, president of Trans-Chemical Corp. They're a hundred-thirty-million-dollar company with plants in New Jersey and Tennessee. Kingsley Smith, their financial V.P., was there, and C. D. Miller, their executive V.P. What's significant here is that Miller recently joined the company. He'd been with Du-Pont. But two months ago he came aboard as executive vice-president."

How a good financial analyst works, how he sizes up a company for investment purposes becomes clear as Stephens talks. "Trans-Chemical is an extremely low-priced stock," he says. "It's been selling about twelve times 1966 earnings, which is very low for a chemical company. The reason is that it has had rather pedestrian management and is in a cyclical business.

"We heard from industry sources that Miller would be a great addition to Trans-Chemical, and we own stock in the company. That is, our growth fund has a position in it: thirty thousand shares worth about seven hundred thousand dollars. So I thought I ought to meet with the new man. And I did—for two hours. It was unusual to get quite that much time with the three top men in the company, but they know they've had a problem. The stock has been under some selling pressure. They're aware of their poor stockholder image, and there was a rumor out that their first-quarter earnings would be flat as against a year ago. So they recognized the importance of meeting with us.

"I usually have my questions prepared beforehand— about management, research, new product development, markets, acquisitions, accounting practices, pricing problems in certain segments of the industry; how the company fits into the over-all industry picture; and what its earnings prospects are for the current year. This time we discussed a possible acquisition program for this year and next; we talked about their strategy in foreign markets—I was particularly interested in that because their foreign income doubled last year. We discussed their decision not to go into plastics.

"I got all the figures and their reasoning. But we are buying managements, not just numbers. So while I'm paying attention to all this, I'm also watching Miller, the new executive V.P. Is he going to make a real difference? Here he is—Phi Beta Kappa, Ph.D. in economics, a director of a company doing space research, and another company that services oil companies in the geological field. He knows his way around. He understands operations research and computer technology. His forte is planning and acquisition.

"I came to the conclusion that he *was* going to bring something to this company that it had never had: a modern, youthful look. If you take all this and put it together, the outlook is positive. The numbers are right and the man is right."

Yet, as Stephens explains, this impression still isn't enough. "Over the weekend," he says, "I put some more numbers together. My evaluation of Trans-Chemical doesn't stop with the interview. What do we know about the competition, about pricing, volume, new products? It's an over-all business evaluation.

"Then, on Monday, I dictate from my skeleton notes. The report only runs about five pages. It concludes with a recommendation: hold Trans-Chemical and build up our position over the next few months—especially if it weakens as a result of first-quarter earnings. Earnings *will* be down, but this drop will be due to several nonrecurring factors.

"This recommendation, of course, is not for *all* our funds. This company would not be appropriate for our balanced fund or even our common stock fund. Dividends are too thin. But dividends aren't as important in our growth fund. To me it's like a well-executed reverse-pass play when a recommendation of mine is accepted and everything works out. There's a sense of craft here. You try to use all the scientific tools, but financial analysis is an art."

EMC's nine analysts travel about 450,000 miles a year in aggregate, collecting detailed data and personal insights about literally hundreds of corporations, including every one held in the portfolio of the Enterprise funds, for it is a house policy at EMC never to buy a security of a company unless that company has been visited first by a financial analyst.

EMC also makes an effort to see that a constant exchange of information occurs among the analysts, the economist, the technical and statistical people. No group works in isolation. At formal meetings, and at informal drop-ins at each other's offices, there is continuing dialogue—more accurately, multilogue. New information, from whatever quarter it comes, is fed into the common reservoir of insight and data.

Intelligence, raw data, refined data, insight, and foresight are the material out of which the actual investment decision is made. Even so, research is only the beginning. The basic decision-making function is carried out by the Investment Committee, the group ultimately responsible for the hundreds of millions of dollars entrusted to EMC's care.

From
Data
to
Decision

Chapter
Nine

O N Tuesday mornings at precisely
nine forty-five a group of men gather around the long,
highly polished mahogany table in the board room of the
Enterprise Management Company. A yellow pad, a mimeographed agenda, and several sharpened pencils are
neatly lined up in front of each chair.

Investment research, no matter how well gathered and
organized, is only useful when applied. Data must be
translated into decision. This is done by a group of five
men who are the company's senior investment policy-
makers. The group is headed, of course, by EMC's president, Wilson Harris. It also includes Clarke, the executive
vice-president; Kramer, head of the investment division;
and Kramer's two chief subordinates, Mitchell, the research director, and Williamson, the portfolio supervisor.*

Investment decisions of the company are confidential.
For this reason, no outside visitors are permitted to attend
Investment Committee meetings. But if one did, he would

* See table of organization, page 78. Each member of the Investment
Policy Committee is marked with an asterisk.

find the five members of the Committee seated near the head of the table. Ranged along its sides are several other members of the EMC staff.

The vice-president in charge of administration is usually present. The economist is there, too, as are several financial analysts. Investment Committee meetings are open to all of EMC's analysts, and they are encouraged to attend and participate. But on any given Tuesday several will be out of town on field trips or other business. Finally, there are three men from Williamson's portfolio department. These three, always present, are called "fund managers." Each has direct personal responsibility for the portfolio of one of the three Enterprise mutual funds.

A typical meeting of the Investment Committee opens with a fifteen-minute report on general business conditions by the economist. When the economist has finished, Harris calls on Portfolio Supervisor Williamson to give a quick review of the money market and the stock market. Williamson perhaps concludes his report by suggesting that increased trading activity may lead to more volatility in the market in the weeks ahead.

Next he outlines the changes made by each of the three Enterprise funds in their portfolios during the past week. He reports, for example, that the balanced fund made purchases of $4.35 million during the week and sold some $5 million worth of portfolio shares, thus coming up with net sales of $650,000. In view of the likelihood of greater shakiness in the stock market, he says, the fund's sales consisted largely of shares of companies in the electronic and office-equipment industries. Its purchases were concentrated in banks and utilities, a more stable grouping. This had the effect of steadying the portfolio—battening the hatches, as it were.

At the same time, the ratio of common stocks in the portfolio was reduced slightly, from 67.8 to 66.3 per cent of assets. This once more represented a move in the direction of stabilization of the portfolio.

After a similar summary of the past week's activities with regard to the Enterprise Common Stock Fund and the Enterprise Growth Fund, Williamson also outlines what is called the "uncompleted program"—the backlog of unexpected buy or sell decisions left over from the preceding week.

Once Williamson is through describing the unfinished business of the three funds, Harris turns to the financial analysts and asks whether anything special has happened in their industries that needs to be brought to the attention of the Committee. One takes the floor briefly to describe a possible merger of two large companies in the textile field. Since the Enterprise Common Stock Fund holds a substantial block of the shares of one of the two companies, the news is of direct relevance.

By ten thirty the first part of the meeting—the data part—is over. At this point, all except the five members of the Investment Committee adjourn. The decision part of the meeting now begins, with the five members weighing what they have heard, fitting the data together with what they themselves have learned in the normal course of their top-level contacts with others in the financial and business community. It is not their function at this meeting to make specific buy and sell recommendations, but rather to set broad policy for the funds.

But what is "broad policy" for a money manager responsible for hundreds of millions of dollars? The answer is best given by the recommendations made by the Investment Committee. The balanced fund now has 66.3 per cent of its assets in common stocks. The Committee moves to reduce this slightly. It decides that an effort should be made "to maintain a common stock position of 63 per cent to 65 per cent." This means that the fund will have to switch about $3 million out of common stocks and into bonds and preferreds. The Committee also decides that, in view of the general agreement that a period of increased volatility lies ahead, the fund should exercise even greater than ordinary caution when it does buy common stock for any reason. Purchases should be "selective and emphasize seasoned issues of investment quality," the Committee declares.

Next, the Committee directs that the balanced fund should also slow up its rate of investment. In addition to the 66.3 per cent now in common stocks, the fund holds 30.0 per cent of its assets in bonds and preferreds. This means, therefore, that the fund now has 96.3 per cent of its assets invested in bonds, preferreds, and common. This leaves 3.7 per cent in cash and government securities. The Committee instructs the fund to allow these reserves to accumulate as new money comes in until they represent 5.6 per cent of the fund's total assets.

This policy is put forward for two reasons. First, it represents another step toward safety and conservatism. Second, by shoring up reserves, it makes available a supply of money that can be used quickly if the coming market fluctuations make some bargain purchases possible.

This is the sort of high policy with which the members of the Investment Committee concern themselves at their Tuesday morning meetings. After issuing a parallel set of recommendations for the Enterprise Growth Fund and the Enterprise Common Stock Fund, the Committee adjourns.

The man responsible for seeing to it that these policies are translated into action is the portfolio supervisor, Williamson. As director of the portfolio department, he has three fund managers under him. When a financial analyst returns from one of his field trips and recommends the purchase of a stock—say Trans-Chemical—the recommendation goes in written form to one or more of the fund managers.

Nobody, however, is bound by this. Explaining the system, James Clarke says: "It's a recommendation and nothing more. In the final analysis, it's Williamson's man, the manager of each fund, who has to decide whether or not he wants to follow it. In this case, the fund manager of the growth fund has to decide whether he wants more Trans-Chemical in his portfolio. If he does, he makes his own recommendation. This goes up to the Investment Committee, and he has to get the consent of at least two members of the Committee. Usually the fund manager takes his recommendation to Williamson, who then collects the additional necessary signatures."

This procedure guarantees that buying and selling will be done in an orderly and responsible fashion, although a decision can be reached in minutes when essential.

"In this set-up," Clarke continues, "the fund manager is really the pivotal person. He is on the frontline. Every week he invests millions of dollars of other people's money. It takes a special kind of guy to do this job well. He can't be impulsive. And he can't be too rigid."

Jeff Stryker is the fund manager in charge of the Enterprise Growth Fund—the smallest of the Enterprise mutual funds, with a portfolio valued at about $75 million. But it is also, by design, the most volatile.

What does a fund manager think about in making his buy and sell decisions? Stryker answers the question this way:

"As a fund manager, my job is to give actual buy and sell orders to our trading room. But, in deciding which recommendations of the analysts to accept, or which to initiate myself, I keep a lot of things in mind.

"First, of course, we're a growth fund. That eliminates a whole lot of stocks right away—perfectly good ones, but stocks that aren't appropriate for our purpose, which is appreciation of capital.

"Second, there's the charter of the fund to think about —the mandate. By the terms of our contracts with the mutual funds to which we act as investment adviser, we have complete responsibility for the management of the portfolios—within limits set by the investment policies and objectives of each fund as set forth in its prospectus. The boards of directors of the funds are the guardians of these policies. They also see to it that we observe these limits. Each fund board member receives reports of our investment actions weekly, and the boards themselves meet monthly. In the case of our own particular approach, they do not enter into the day-to-day investment activities; and we feel that this, in fact, gives them better perspective when it comes time to review our performance. Key sections of the charter are printed in the prospectus we distribute to the shareholders, and it contains a set of rules telling what we can and cannot do with their money." Here he reaches into his top desk drawer, fishes out a folder, and reads aloud:

"The Fund may not invest in the securities of companies which, including predecessors, do not have a record of at least three years' continuous operation." This, he takes pains to point out, is different from the stipulation that appears in the charter of the other two funds in the house. The common stock fund cannot invest in a company less than five years old; the balanced fund, the most conservative of the three, requires that a company be seven years old before its shares become eligible for inclusion in the portfolio.

Beyond this, Stryker observes, "I can't concentrate more than twenty-five per cent of my portfolio in any one industry. I can't buy or sell commodity futures, or commodities. No margin transactions are permitted, no short sales, and so forth. It's all spelled out in the charter."

The charter lays down basic ground rules. But there are also unwritten rules Stryker must observe: "Every fund develops a character of its own, a particular style that its shareholders come to expect. So that on any proposed transaction you begin to think very much whether this is in keeping with what your fifteen thousand shareholders have come to expect of you."

Next, Stryker says, "there are the policy lines laid down by the Investment Committee. If the investment policy committee is taking a bearish view of things, I have to take that into account."

In addition Stryker is bound by all the normal considerations that anyone investing in corporate stocks must bear in mind. "I watch the rate of growth of the company we're considering. The amount of risk. Its position in the industry. The quality of its management. The relative attractiveness of this stock as compared with others in the same industry. And even after we've made up our mind about the company, we have to make sure that it fits into the general composition of the portfolio. Composition is important.

"Currently, we like to have about fifteen per cent of the portfolio in petroleum-company stocks. We tend to keep something like ten per cent in business-machines companies—Xerox, Burroughs, IBM. We'll usually put another ten per cent or so in electronics. We carry Ampex, Texas Instruments, Fairchild Camera in the portfolio, to name a few. After that, we pretty much limit our commitment in any one company to about five per cent of the portfolio or less. Altogether, we have ninety-five companies in seventeen different industry groups represented in the portfolio, and we keep them more or less in a given balance. So that we really do diversify, and any buy or sell recommendation has to be considered from the point of view of its impact on the general composition of the portfolio."

Such considerations lie in the back of the fund manager's mind when he consults—as he does several times a day—with individual financial analysts. While many of the buy or sell "ideas" originate with analysts, others are initiated by Stryker, his superior Williamson, or by individual members of the Investment Committee. Regardless of origin, in each case the fund manager checks them out with the analyst responsible for the industry involved.

Since the fund manager buys and sells millions of dollars worth of stock every week, many brokers call him directly, urging this or that stock on him. He attempts to insulate himself from some of these calls by shunting them to the appropriate analyst. He takes only calls from brokers he has come to know over the years as being particularly astute. Indeed, he keeps an informal record in his card file of the ideas any individual broker presents to him.

"Sure," he explains, "when you talk with a broker, he'll remind you of the ideas he gave you in the past that paid off. But he obviously won't very often remind you of the ideas he had that didn't work. So whether we follow up on the ideas or not, I usually keep a few penciled notes on his card. That way I can evaluate his performance as an idea man over a period of time. I know the ones who come up with consistently good ideas and those who don't."

The fund manager, occupying a critical spot in the mutual fund organization, has wide discretion to shape the portfolio of the fund under his management. His "output" consists of orders telling the trading room which securities to buy or sell. He also establishes the price range within which the trading room may act. On Trans-Chemical, for example, the fund manager of the Enterprise Growth Fund might tell the trading room that he wants a block of 30,000 additional shares, but wants to pick them up at 23⅝ or less.

Up to this point, a series of internal decisions has been made. Data have been converted into decisions. It is the market specialist at work in the trading department who now converts these decisions into action.

When a fund wishes to buy or sell securities for its portfolio, it places an order with a brokerage firm. The broker receives a commission for executing the transaction. Often a fund will take its portfolio business to a brokerage firm that is also engaged in selling the fund's own shares to the public. Commissions may also be used to reward brokerage firms that provide special services—for example, helping the fund price its portfolio daily or offering investment research assistance to the fund adviser. But the trading department has a primary responsibility to place its buy and sell orders for portfolio transactions where the best prices and executions can be obtained for the fund. And to do so, it must stay in constant touch with the various securities markets.

The trading room is a spacious office that contains three desks carefully lined up side by side so that their tops form a single long surface. Along this surface runs a single continuous metal track. At one end of the room a ticker tape spews out a ribbon of paper on which the latest stock prices are printed. This ribbon floats silently along the track in front of each of the three market specialists before it falls in a curly mass into a basket next to the desk on the far left.

The chief of the trading department maintains a "blotter"—a working list of buys and sells to be consummated. It lists the exact time at which the trading department received its instructions from the fund managers, the price range within which each of the stocks on the list fluctuated the day before, the number of shares bought and sold by the Enterprise funds the day before.

A trader or "market specialist" must be able to sense even minor currents in the market. He must be skilled at timing, knowing when to be aggressive and when to pull back and wait. He must know not only what he wants to buy or sell, and the appropriate prices, but also how to avoid "being the market" when this might have the effect of driving up the price of a stock on the "buy" list or driving a price down when the fund wishes to sell.

"Being the market" is being the dominant buyer or seller for some particular stock at any given point. Thus the Enterprise people must know what is happening in the various markets and be able to act quickly on behalf

of their funds. Not surprisingly, the trading-room tele-
phones keep ringing. The chief trader alone may take or
place as many as seventy-five or a hundred calls daily as
various brokers check in and he and his subordinates feed
the orders out.

In this way, at last, the data provided by the research
department, the policies laid down by the Investment
Committee, and the directives of the fund managers are
fitted together bit by bit into a pattern. An investment
program is created professionally, not haphazardly. Portfolios are built, modified, dynamically reconstructed again
and again to serve the objective of each fund.

The investment function is the heart of any sponsor
company. Yet managing money is more than just buying
and selling shares. There is an entirely different side to the
work done by the Enterprise Management Company for
the three funds it advises.

Beyond

Chapter # Investment

Ten

Imagine a mutual fund that employs the best investment brains in the country and regularly outperforms all other mutual funds of its type. Yet when a shareholder writes in to find out how much he has in his account he receives a letter stating that, owing to a slight mix-up, the fund has no way of answering his question. At the end of the year he receives a capital gains distribution, but the fund fails to make plain how much of it represents long-term gains, thus making it impossible for him to make out his personal income tax return properly. When he makes a purchase, the shares are issued in the wrong name and at the wrong address. When he receives dividends, he gets a check covering the amount due on 350 or 750 shares in spite of the fact that he actually holds 400 shares.

There is of course no such fund, for no mutual fund could survive if it handled other people's money so cavalierly. It is unlikely that any shareholder would be willing to keep his money in such a fund for any length of time because he could have no confidence in the competence, reliability, probity (or even, perhaps, the sanity) of the men running it. In short, it takes more than investment know-how to operate a mutual fund; it takes a high degree of administrative and record-keeping skill as well.

"There is a tendency," Enterprise's executive vice-president explains, "to talk about mutual fund advisers as if all they did was research and supervise a portfolio. Yet with seventy thousand shareholders in the three Enterprise funds, we have every bit as much corporate administration as any other big company. There is an immense amount of correspondence, all kinds of accounting to be done, reports to be filed with regulatory and tax agencies, agendas to be worked up, meetings to be held, minutes to be kept. Enterprise Management takes this administrative load off the three Enterprise funds. The funds, in paying us that one-half of one per cent management fee, not only buy our investment and research and advice, they also buy a complete package of administrative services.

"No one on the outside has any idea of the paper superstructure here. A lot of it has to do with safeguarding the customer and his investment and keeping him informed and up to date. A lot of work goes into the seemingly simple chore of record-keeping on all these thousands of accounts and transactions, so we know at any moment how much there is in any individual account."

Clarke's words are underscored by the comment of an official of one leading fund. This fund underwent a period of sharp growth in the late 1950's, with almost disastrous results. In a period of a few years its number of shareholders rose from 80,000 to 300,000. The fund's adviser company employed 100 girls to operate 50 bookkeeping machines on a two-shift-a-day basis to keep up with the records, but it was inundated. To have attempted to keep up, as the number of shareholders increased, would have required a battery of 500 machines and hundreds of girls. A fund official said: "There would have been sheer chaos here if we had tried to keep up with the work in the old way. We simply had to switch to a computer operation."

Nothing like chaos has threatened the Enterprise funds, but several years ago EMC had the foresight to begin the computerization of its record-keeping. Today EMC leases an IBM 1401 and is planning to install an IBM 1410.

"Twice a day," says James Clarke, "the prices of each of our portfolio securities are phoned in and key-punched onto cards. Within one minute of the time they are fed into the machine we get our pricing. We know the exact value of each of the three Enterprise fund portfolios as of that time, and the net asset value of each individual Enterprise fund share."

The computer is also used to speed confirmations. If a customer wishes to buy or redeem shares of an Enterprise fund, his transaction is processed overnight and a letter of confirmation is on its way to him the following morning.

"This machine," Clarke continues, "handles only part of the job. We also make use of an IBM 1410 that belongs to our bank. That's where the actual account records are maintained, and the transactions are processed and re-corded."

While computerization is helping EMC cope with the rising tide of essential record-keeping, the administrative operation of a mutual fund cannot be completely mecha-nized. The company, for example, receives a daily ava-lanche of mail. Apart from orders and redemptions, there are letters requesting changes in the plan or type of account, changes in the name of the account holder, changes in address; there are letters requesting informa-tion about services, about share value, about fund poli-cies, and prospects. Only some of these can be answered with form replies.

A leading mutual fund received a note from one of its shareholders. The writer, an irate lady from Chicago, had

bought an electric toaster bearing the trademark of one of
the nation's leading appliance makers. On taking it home,
she found to her surprise that the toaster was defective.
The woman thereupon phoned the retailer who had sold
it, requesting a new machine. The retailer refused. Irri-
tated, she called the manufacturer's local service office
and demanded satisfaction. Once again nothing happened. By now she was furious; she wrote to her mutual
fund, saying, "since you own 20,000 shares of the company that built this thing, I think you ought to help a
shareholder get her money back or her machine fixed."

Mutual funds are not in the business of settling disputes
between companies and their customers, but they are
highly sensitive to the wishes of their shareholders. The
fund forwarded a copy of the letter to the manufacturer,
along with a suggestion that the matter be looked into.

The next link in the chain of correspondence was a
rapturous letter from the lady. "I got my new toaster," she
exulted, "delivered right to my door, by hand, by a vice-
president himself."

Not all stockholder requests are so easily answered. An
elderly shareholder in Oklahoma wrote to the same fund
asking for a duplicate stock certificate. From what he
wrote and from what was evident between the lines, he
had kept his stock certificate in a safe-deposit box at a
local bank. Being inordinately suspicious of financial people, however, he had gone to the bank every day to see if
it was still there. The old man had apparently gotten on
everyone's nerves and he was asked to take his business
elsewhere. His letter to the fund explained, "I thought of
having a safe put in my house, but I figured if I could
put it in, someone else could get it out." So instead he
carried his certificate with him everywhere he went, wrap-

ping it in tissue to keep it from wearing out. The fund could not send him a duplicate, for a stock certificate cannot be replaced unless lost or destroyed.

Other letters arrive at various mutual funds from shareholders who object, on moral or religious grounds, to fund ownership of shares of tobacco or liquor companies. Some shareholders demand that their fund divest itself of shares of chemical companies that make fluorides or participate in the manufacture of chemical warfare products. Others complain that this or that portfolio company's television advertising is noxious.

Some shareholders consider themselves stock market experts and offer investment advice to their funds. Others tout a particular stock, and now and then a shareholder will urge the fund to invest in some dubious oil-exploration deal in Brazil or Borneo. One man pushing a zany investment venture wrote his fund a postcard each week for months.

Such relatively offbeat letters, of course, make up only a tiny minority of the thousands of letters received in any year by any large fund, but they serve to illustrate, and to remind fund officials, that shareholders are not numbers, but people.

The Sale of Shares

Chapter Eleven

Every year Americans from La Jolla, California, to LaGrangeville, New York, buy billions of dollars worth of mutual fund shares. Year after year, as new millions learn about the mutual fund method, the number of shares held by the public continues to rise. What is the mechanism by which these shares reach the shareholder? How, in short, are mutual fund shares sold?

These shares are distributed in various ways. The most common system, accounting for some 60 per cent of all sales, can be illustrated by once again examining the mythical Enterprise funds. The sponsoring organization, Enterprise Management, has (in addition to an investment division and an administrative division) a third arm—a wholly owned subsidiary called Enterprise Fund Distributors, Inc. This arm of the company has the task of wholesaling shares of the Enterprise funds through securities dealers and brokers all over the country who offer them for sale to the public, exactly as they offer the shares of other mutual funds and corporate securities.

Harry Wright, the president of Enterprise Fund Distributors, describes his function: "Ours is the distributing organization for Enterprise shares; we are the wholesalers. We have seventeen field men based throughout the U.S. They call on investment dealers and brokers and brief them on the three Enterprise funds, suggesting how they should be sold to the public and how to match the objectives of the fund with those of the individual investor. In the case of the Enterprise Balanced Fund, for example, our objectives are principally conservation of capital, reasonable income, and reasonable appreciation without undue risk. This might not be the appropriate investment goal for a young couple; it might be just right for an older couple. We discuss this with the dealers and brokers. We explain the various services we offer, the reinvestment features, the reduced schedule of fees for large orders, and so on.

"We also have a financial planning department that will assist any dealer in analyzing a specific investor's problem. If he has certain things he wants to accomplish in a given period of time, if he wants to set up a profit-sharing program, retirement plans, pensions, our men will help the dealer or broker help the investor. Sometimes we will send a man from our financial planning department out to work with a dealer or broker, with the customer and the customer's lawyer and accountant, to put together an investment program to cover deferred compensation for executives, salary-deduction plans for the employees, and so forth."

Last year, Wright says, Enterprise Fund Distributors, Inc., sold $40 million worth of Enterprise fund shares. These shares carried a sales charge of from 8 per cent down to 2 per cent, depending upon the size of the purchase order. In practice, the average commission worked out to slightly over 6 per cent. This meant that the sale of Enterprise shares generated about $2.4 million in commissions. Of this sum, three fourths or $1.8 million remained with the brokers and dealers. The remaining $600,000 represented the gross income of Enterprise Fund Distributors, Inc. This money paid for the seventeen field men, for the financial planning specialists, for printing and literature, and for general overhead. The company, after all these expenses, showed a small profit, which it contributed to the over-all income of the parent company, Enterprise Management Company, Inc. This small profit, as a matter of fact, was a tribute to Wright's tight management; as a rule, the wholesale distribution of mutual fund shares is not profitable for the fund sponsor until it reaches a volume of $60 million to $70 million worth of shares per year. Even then sales may prove unprofitable for the sponsor. In the words of *Dun's Review*, "It is no secret that the sponsors of many leading funds make little or no money on the sales commission. . . . They tend to plow what they do earn back into more sales promotion."

The sale of Enterprise shares at the retail level is carried out by brokers and dealers across the country, with whom Enterprise Fund Distributors, Inc., has contracts. These contracts are nonexclusive franchises that permit the broker or dealer to sell Enterprise shares to the public under certain terms. Most broker-dealers handle a wide range of corporate securities as well as the shares of many different mutual funds.

The Securities and Exchange Commission in 1962 found that, of nearly 5000 broker-dealer firms registered with it, 1555 reported the sale of mutual fund shares as their primary business. Another 612 listed mutual fund sales as a secondary activity. Firms like these employ some 80,000 individual salesmen at offices in all major cities in the U.S. These salesmen are there to counsel prospective investors as to which particular fund or which plan would be most appropriate.

How well-trained these broker-dealer salesmen are varies from firm to firm and man to man. But as mutual fund sales have become increasingly important, some securities retailers have begun specialized training programs to prepare their salesmen. One leading brokerage firm, for example, now has a mutual fund department which, in the words of its manager, "is responsible for training, educating, stimulating, and encouraging salesmen to sell mutual funds." The training involves special classes and seminars devoted to the problems and potentials of the mutual fund method of investing. Most major brokerage firms carry out similar programs.

This system, in which a distributor (also called a wholesaler or underwriter) stands in some organic relationship to the fund adviser and pipes fund shares into the retail network of brokerage offices and dealerships, is typical of much of the mutual fund industry.

Some funds—the so-called no-loads—employ a second system. As we have seen, they normally make little or no active effort to sell shares. Since these funds charge no sales commission, they usually employ no sales staff. The prospective shareholder generally must write or phone the fund directly to place orders for purchase or redemption.

A third system for the distribution of mutual fund shares is direct selling. Under this system, the fund sponsor sets up a retail sales force. This may consist of hundreds of salesmen. The distributor of the largest U.S. fund today employs about 4000 full-time salesmen, who ordinarily sell nothing but the shares of a single group of funds, although some also handle life insurance. Some funds sell both through broker-dealers *and* through their own sales force.

The sale of mutual fund shares, like that of any investment service, is a rather personal affair. It often involves face-to-face conversation during which the buyer is called upon to discuss financial and family matters that ordinarily remain confidential. It is obvious that in such circumstances it is important to maintain high standards of ethical conduct on the part of the seller. It is also obvious that, with thousands of men and women engaged in the sale of mutual fund shares, there are bound to be a certain number of cases of misunderstanding and a certain incidence of improper, perhaps even unethical, selling, as critics of the fund industry have pointed out on occasion.

While readily agreeing that this may be so, most fund leaders believe that the overwhelming majority of mutual fund transactions meet the highest ethical standards, and they call attention to the volume of mail they receive from satisfied shareholders as evidence. Moreover, they point out, all sales representatives of broker-dealer firms are registered with either the Securities and Exchange Commission or the National Association of Securities Dealers, both of which keep a watchful eye on fund activities.

It is important to understand that, whatever system of distribution is used, sales are the lifeblood of most mutual funds. Sales are important to the fund adviser for the obvious reason that any increase in the size of the funds under its management brings with it an increase in the size of the management fee. But sales also serve another purpose. They represent a fresh flow of money into the fund and contribute to its healthy growth. New money from sales does two things: it provides cash with which to take advantage of market opportunities and, at the same time, it reduces the amount of cash reserve necessary to meet redemption requirements. This means that the funds are able to put a higher percentage of their total assets in the productive part of the portfolio. This, in turn, is of benefit to every shareholder, old or new.

These chapters have attempted to present a picture of the inner workings of a more or less typical mutual fund group. All funds and all sponsors differ from one another in details of organization, structure, philosophical approach, degree of professionalism, and degree of formality or informality with which they operate. Nevertheless, we can look upon the Enterprise funds as being more or less representative. Most funds are what the Enterprise funds are—legal entities created and served by a sponsoring organization. All advisers must, in one way or another, conduct investment research; all must have some machinery for converting investment decisions into actual portfolio purchases and sales; all must perform or arrange to have performed a wide range of administrative services; all must funnel their shares to the public through one sales mechanism or another. If the mythical Enterprise funds and the Enterprise Management Company, Inc., have served to make this clear, they have accomplished their purpose and may now be retired from this book.

Part Three

MONEY
AND THE
MARKETPLACE

Safeguards for Shareholders

Chapter Twelve

M UTUAL FUNDS "are probably the most closely regulated sector of the entire securities business . . . the laws enacted to prevent possible abuses of trust are clear-cut and far-reaching . . . they represent a plus factor not obtainable in any comparable investment medium." This is the opinion of the Wiesenberger annual, *Investment Companies.* What it means is that there are a lot of rules with which mutual funds must comply, rules that help safeguard the shareholder.

Mutual funds are not only regulated by the Securities and Exchange Commission; in order to be eligible for beneficial tax treatment, they must also meet certain requirements of the Internal Revenue Code. Moreover, they are subject at the state level to a maze of laws and regulations administered by various state authorities charged with watchdogging the sale and distribution of securities. In addition to all this, the Investment Company Institute, the industry association, while it lacks regulatory power, has issued a *Guide to Business Standards* that sets out certain ethical criteria for the industry.

In 1911—many years before the first mutual fund was formed—Kansas became the first state to pass a law providing for the registration of securities and securities salesmen. Since then almost all states have enacted laws regulating the sale of securities. The result is a webwork of laws and administrative rules that keep staffs of lawyers busy in and outside the mutual fund industry. It is impossible to summarize all these rules and regulations here —they vary greatly from state to state. But they touch on everything from sales methods and commissions to operating costs and diversification policies.

Moreover, since most funds operate nationally, they often find it necessary to comply with the toughest laws on the books. For example, Ohio has a rule (called Regulation Q-3) that prohibits a fund from investing more than 5 per cent of its assets in a single company or from buying up more than 10 per cent of the securities of any single company. The federal requirement on this point is less restrictive. But since most funds want to sell their shares in Ohio, they choose to comply with the state regulation even though it is stiffer than the federal law on the same point.

But state regulations are only part of the picture. The real story begins with the passage of the Federal Securities Act of 1933 and the Federal Securities Exchange Act of 1934. These two laws were not designed solely with mutual funds in mind. They were general legislation intended to bring the securities industry as a whole under federal surveillance. But their provisions influence mutual funds deeply.

The chief purpose of the 1933 act was to see that there was full and fair disclosure of the character of any securities sold in interstate commerce. Speculative securities could be sold. The government did not pass on the merit of any security. It merely required that the potential investor be told what he is buying. The act requires mutual funds (or any other company issuing shares to the public) to furnish the public with a detailed and accurate prospectus and to file a registration statement with the SEC.

The 1934 act went much further. While the legislation of the year before was aimed at protecting investors in the purchase of *newly issued* securities, the 1934 law was intended to safeguard the investor in brokerage transactions involving the buying or selling of *outstanding* securities. This is not the place for a detailed explanation of how, through this piece of landmark legislation, the federal government today regulates stock exchanges, brokers, dealers, borrowing and margin requirements, proxies and their solicitation, and many other aspects of the securities industry. Suffice it to say that this is the basic law of the land with respect to investment in securities. Its purpose and tone may be summed up by quoting a single paragraph from a ruling issued under the act. This is Rule 10b-5, which makes it a federal offense, through interstate commerce, through the mails, or through any national stock exchange:

(1) to employ any device, scheme, or artifice to defraud, (2) to make any untrue statement of a material fact or to omit to state a material fact necessary in order to make the statements made, in the light of the circumstances under which they were made, not misleading, or (3) to engage in any act, practice, or course of business which operates or would operate as a fraud or deceit upon any person, in connection with the purchase or sale of any security.

Together these two laws "unquestionably gave the general public a generous measure of the protection that they had long deserved"—so says the president of a leading fund sponsor. But, as already noted, both these acts were

general in their application. It was six more years before
Congress passed the law that has come to be called the
Magna Carta of the mutual funds, the Investment Com-
pany Act of 1940.

This law was based on years of investigation, hearings,
discussion with industry leaders, skillful drafting and re-
drafting. In its final form it had solid backing not only
from the SEC, which administers it, but from the mutual
fund men as well. They recognized that intelligent federal
regulation would help, not harm, the industry.

The Investment Company Act of 1940 runs to forty-
seven pages of print. Point by point, it covers almost every
aspect of fund operation. At each step, its wording is
intended to protect the shareholder from possible abuse.

Like the earlier legislation, it requires funds to register,
and to file a comprehensive statement with the SEC
detailing their policies with regard to borrowing, the
issuance of senior securities, concentration of investments
in particular industries, lending money, and so forth.
These policies, once registered, cannot be changed except
with the approval of the shareholders.

The importance of this requirement is clear. It means
that a shareholder gets what he is promised in the way of
fund policy. It means he will not wake up some morning
to find that, without notifying him, the fund is now
following policies different from those in force at the time
his investment was made. Thus an elderly couple that
invests in a balanced fund because it offers conservation
of capital and modest income will not suddenly find their
money being invested by the fund in a high-risk growth
portfolio. Nor, if the fund claims to be a diversified fund,
will they find that it has invested a third or a half of its

assets in a single company or industry. In short, the fund must pursue the fundamental policies it sets forth in its prospectus. It cannot change those policies without shareholders' consent.

The 1940 legislation also stipulates that at least 40 per cent of the directors of any mutual fund (except for a no-load fund meeting certain requirements) must be independent—totally unaffiliated with the fund's investment adviser. No fund is permitted to sell its shares to anyone at a price less than the current net asset value per share. This means that a fund may not dilute the value of its existing shares by selling new shares at less than their current value. Moreover, "affiliated" persons—insiders—generally cannot buy portfolio securities from the fund or sell securities to it (a restriction designed to eliminate the possibility that someone in the adviser firm will be able to "dump" unsalable stocks on a fund, or buy stocks from it at advantageous prices). Furthermore, mutual funds may not as a rule acquire a substantial block of the stock of other investment companies. They cannot become involved in the kind of "pyramiding" that led to the pile up of one holding company atop another during the pre-crash 1920's.

The contract between a fund and its investment adviser is also regulated. It must be approved at the outset by the shareholders, and cannot initially run for more than two years. After that it must be approved annually by a majority of the board of directors of the fund, including a majority of the independent directors, or by the shareholders themselves. Most important, the contract is non-transferable. That is, it is automatically terminated if the adviser assigns it. In other words, a shareholder who in-

vests in a fund because he wants the investment advice of
Adviser A will not suddenly find that his fund is actually
being serviced by Adviser B.

As for payout to shareholders, no mutual fund may issue
a dividend without a clear statement as to the source of
the dividend money.

There are page after page of additional provisions in
the Investment Company Act of 1940, covering items as
specific as the names mutual funds may choose.

The SEC's heavy emphasis on complete disclosure has
meant that the mutual fund industry has operated in a
goldfish bowl. No other sector of the investment industry
puts more information on public record. Recently, the
SEC introduced a new reporting requirement. Called
"Form N–1R," this is a sixty-four-page form that each fund
must file each year. It covers every aspect of operations,
from breakdown of expenses and portfolio turnover rates
to the remuneration of officers of sponsor companies. Says
a former Attorney General of the United States, now counsel to a leading mutual fund: "No industry I know of does
everything in Macy's store window the way this one does.
It's all public knowledge."

Looking back at the enactment of the Investment Company Act of 1940, one historian has said: "It cleared the
atmosphere; it codified the rules of the game." Abuses
that had sprung up in the early days of the industry were
eliminated. Subsequent refinements of the law and its
administration have further strengthened the protection
available to the shareholder. In the words of *Fortune:* "The
Investment Company Act of 1940 . . . goes about as far
as any law can toward taming a financial enterprise
whose main function is to deal in risk capital. The law
requires safeguards much stricter than the full-disclosure

requirements that apply to offers of other types of securities. The SEC has a life-and-death power over growth of a fund. . . ."

The state authorities and the SEC, however, are not the only regulatory forces in the mutual fund industry. The National Association of Securities Dealers is a quasi-governmental agency whose membership includes almost all investment banking houses, brokers, and dealers in the United States. It operates under strict rules intended to maintain high ethical standards in the investment industry generally, and it has the power to expel from membership any firm or individual found guilty of unfair or unethical conduct.

Every individual engaged in selling mutual fund shares is subject to the disciplines of the SEC. In addition, many mutual fund salesmen are subject to the regulation of the NASD and the various state agencies having jurisdiction over securities and their sale.

In a Statement of Policy issued in 1950, the SEC laid down exacting rules covering all advertising and promotional literature in the mutual fund industry. This Statement of Policy is enforced by the NASD, and funds submit advertising brochures and other sales aids to the NASD for clearance. Early in the century the advertisement of stocks and bonds was a wild and woolly business. Such phrases as "an investment protected by 400 seasoned securities" or "the uncertainty of selecting the profitable companies of the future has been overcome" were common. Today, in the mutual fund field especially, restraint and accuracy are the key words.

All prospectuses and brochures caution the potential investor that funds cannot guarantee success. Funds may not "represent or imply an assurance that an investor will receive a stable, continuous, dependable, or liberal return or that he will receive any specified rate or rates of return." They may not mention that funds are regulated by the federal government or the states without explicitly pointing out that this does not involve federal or state supervision of management and investment policies or practices.

Charts, graphs, statistical compilations are all subject to precise restrictions that prevent deception. Any statements that encourage an investor to switch from one fund to another must be accompanied by a paragraph pointing out that doing so may involve additional sales commissions.

According to *Fortune,* "Regulations on advertising claims are so strict that some members of the industry wonder how they manage to sell fund shares at all." The magazine quotes one industry leader as commenting: "Suppose the real-estate industry had to sell houses the way we sell shares. If they were under the same requirements, house-for-sale ads might have to read: 'For Sale. A House. Nice neighborhood, but this is not meant to indicate that the neighborhood could not change. Sound construction, but this is no guarantee that the house might not fall down at any moment. Inquiries invited."

This, on the other hand, is not meant to suggest that the industry would like all restrictions on sales and promotion literature lifted. While specific requirements may sometimes chafe those who have to prepare sales literature, most mutual fund leaders today are publicly on record as favoring realistic safeguards. Says the executive vice-president of one of the major sponsor firms: "Good regulation of the business is a plus—even in a sales effort."

Recently, the S.E.C. completed the first comprehensive

study of the mutual fund industry since 1940. The results of this study were set forth in a report to Congress in which recommendations were made for additional legislation dealing with the regulation of the mutual fund industry. The decision with respect to these recommendations is pending before Congress.

In addition to all this, the Investment Company Institute, the association of mutual funds, can and does apply continuing moral suasion in an effort to maintain high ethical standards in the industry. While the Institute has no power to regulate its members, its *Guide to Business Standards* establishes a general code of conduct with respect to the private dealings of employees of funds or adviser organizations. For example, it declares: "No person should seek or accept favors or preferential treatment from broker-dealers because of his association with an investment company." The influence of the Institute thus helps mold the house rules applied by funds and adviser firms to their own employees.

Of course, no house policy, no industry association's ethical code, not even the rules and regulations of state and federal agencies can guarantee absolute honesty in any industry. One hundred per cent compliance with high standards, 100 per cent honesty, is an ideal.

Yet, as this chapter has made plain, the mutual fund industry operates within a fine tracery of legal and moral strictures. It is unlikely any serious wrongdoing could continue for long. This web of laws, administrative rulings, and ethical codes is itself constantly being revised, articulated, and tightened. In no other comparable investment field will the shareholder find so many safeguards.

Economic
Chapter Impact
Thirteen

ON Monday, May 28, 1962, the Dow-
Jones Average of thirty leading industrial stocks dropped
34.95 points—the sharpest decline since October 28, 1929,
the day of the Great Crash. The volume of shares traded
on the New York Stock Exchange reached 9.35 million,
and the ticker tape that records stock prices was so over-
whelmed that by the close of the day it was running an
hour and nine minutes late. All through the day a sense
of crisis intensified. On that single day alone the value of
stocks listed on the Exchange lost $20.8 billion. As John
Brooks, who described the event in *The New Yorker,* put
it: "In effect, the United States has lost something like
two weeks' worth of products and pay in one day."

But worse was to come. During the first few hours of
May 29 several billion dollars worth of additional value
was erased as stocks continued their precipitous decline.
"The panic was in full cry," wrote Brooks. "And along
with panic came near chaos. . . . May 29th . . . will be
long remembered as the day when there was something
very close to a complete breakdown in the reticulated,
automated, mind-boggling complex of technical facilities
that makes nationwide stock trading possible."

Crowds of tense and anxious investors jammed brokers'
offices. Telephone switchboards were swamped. Radio
and television newscasters, reporting the crisis, sent fear

radiating into every corner of the country. In Milan, Brussels, London, and Zürich stock exchanges, reacting to the news from New York, watched prices spiral downward.

Yet, when the market closed that Tuesday, nearly $13.5 billion of the previous day's losses had been restored. By Thursday evening, the rally was so complete that the indices actually closed higher than they had been before the abrupt, frightening nosedive began.

Behind this remarkable recovery stands a story that sheds light on the importance of mutual funds in the nation's investment system.

Any economy needs capital for growth. Just how much capital is required is suggested by the observation of G. Keith Funston, president of the New York Stock Exchange, that between 1955 and 1964 American nonfinancial corporations "spent slightly more than half a trillion dollars in their business—over $500 billion—primarily to finance the replacement of worn-out or outmoded plant and equipment, and to expand productive capacities."

About 60 per cent of this grand total, some $311 billion, was generated internally by industry itself. This much represented profits plowed back and funds recaptured through allowances for depreciation. But American business still needed to find nearly $200 billion to finance its growth. It obtained this money from various sources. It borrowed from banks and insurance companies; it gave mortgages on property it already held. This borrowing brought about $132 billion. For the remaining $68 billion business turned to the stock market. It is the function of the stock market to provide a meeting place not merely for buyers and sellers of outstanding (already issued) securities, but also for those of new issues of stocks and bonds as well.

Mutual funds do not generally invest their shareholders' money in new and untested securities, and have been criticized for their conservatism. The authors of a study that appeared in *Private Financial Institutions*, a series of research papers prepared for the Commission on Money and Credit, charge that the funds "still do not allocate their funds to smaller firms as much as is desirable. . . ."

What this criticism overlooks is the secondary impact of the funds on the stock market. For, while they may not themselves directly put up risk capital for new ventures, they do reach out and bring new money into the stock market. They invest this new money, as a rule, in outstanding high-grade securities and thereby free other capital that can be used for the support of new ventures.

Professor Edward Marcus, writing in the *Commercial and Financial Chronicle*, suggests:

Much of the investment money that does go into mutuals would not go into equities [stocks] if the mutuals did not exist. Since this is supplied by the small saver who in general is unsophisticated in the ways of Wall Street, it would seem that in the absence of mutuals, the supply of such savings would go into savings banks and other types of savings accounts. Thus, the money would probably be funneled instead into fixed interest securities, such as bonds and mortgages. In contrast, the mutuals would be buyers of equities to a far greater extent. We can thus conclude that the presence of these funds has increased the demand for common stocks.

Since the mutuals are buyers, someone must have been selling. . . . What did the seller . . . do with his proceeds? Some probably went into fixed debt, but it is also probable that a good bit stayed in equities. The movement of mutuals into better quality equities, in other words, probably released a substantial part of the sellers' funds, for venture capital purposes, into the smaller, newer, higher risk industrial companies.

Mutual funds can thus be said to be an important mechanism in the formation of pools of capital for economic growth.

Another interesting effect of mutual fund activity derives from the increased importance of voluntary and contractual plans involving periodic investment. Under these mutual fund investment programs, the shareholder adds to his account regularly over a period of years, in good years and bad, whether the market is up or down. What this means is that part of the mutual fund money entering the stock market arrives in the form of a steady, predictable stream rather than in wild spurts. While this effect may be quite small, it is nevertheless a stabilizing influence on the market.

But the funds affect the stability of the market in various ways. During the Great Crash of 1929, mutual funds were so small as to be almost negligible as a factor in the stock market. But after the Second World War, as the funds grew larger and larger, some stock market observers became alarmed by their potential impact on a declining market. It became almost an article of faith among certain writers that in any serious market shakeout the first investors to sell would be the "small people" with holdings in mutual fund shares. Here is how Louis Engel, in *How to Buy Stocks,* explained the situation as he and other pessimistic prophets saw it:

The big worry about mutual funds today is . . . a matter of economics. How stable would they prove to be in another period of economic stress? Would the big bubble burst again? This is a legitimate worry, because in the structure of most mutual funds there is one contradiction that can spell trouble.

[This trouble lies in the] dangerous . . . situation that might exist if the market went into a tailspin. That's the time when people who owned shares in a mutual fund would be most tempted to cash them in, for that is when they as individuals of generally modest means would be most likely to need their savings. And yet that is precisely the time when it would be most difficult for a mutual fund to redeem its shares, because to raise cash, it would probably have to sell stocks from its portfolio . . . if there were a heavy run on a [fund] it would have to sell off sizable blocks of stock to raise cash and it might very well have to take a loss on those forced sales. Additionally, those very sales might further depress the market.

It was this potential snowball effect that worried many people, including Wall Street sophisticates. Even Engel admitted that the funds had "performed creditably" during market declines in 1946, 1950, 1957, and 1960. In each of these years sales ran ahead of redemptions. But these, Engel declared, "were not really severe tests" of the snowball principle.

What might be called a really severe test came in 1962, by which time, according to John Brooks, "the mere thought of the mutual fund situation was enough" to make many Wall Streeters shudder. As Brooks put it, if the $23 billion then held by the funds, or even any substantial part of it, "were to be tossed onto the market . . . it could generate a crash that would make 1929 seem like a stumble."

What actually happened was just the reverse. The mutual funds, instead of driving the market down in the direction it was already going, played a very important counterbalancing role. Brooks' detailed and colorful account of the 1962 crisis concludes: "The role of the hero was filled, surprisingly, by that most frightening of untested forces in the market—the mutual funds." He then cites statistics, issued by the New York Stock Exchange after an intensive study of the events of that critical week, to show that on Monday (when stock prices were plunging) the funds actually purchased 530,000 more shares than they sold. By Thursday, when the market was rocketing upward again, the funds *sold* 375,000 shares. In other words, Brooks reports, "far from increasing the market's fluctuation, the funds actually served as a stabilizing force."

At a moment when tens of thousands of investors were selling at low prices, fund managers coolly bought; a few days later, when prices had climbed, they sold. They did not necessarily sell the same shares. In fact, since most funds hold for the long term, it is probable that what they sold were not the same shares, but others among the weaker ones in their portfolios. In short, the steady hand of the professional manager was at work, not only taking advantage of the situation for his shareholders but also—by the very act—restoring some sense of order and control to the market place.

At the same time, what were mutual fund shareholders doing? Were they, as had been predicted, clamoring to redeem their shares? Some were. But, at the same time, and in greater numbers, others were buying into the funds. For example, as later figures showed, during the month that saw this dramatic break some 40,000 individuals opened new accumulation plans with mutual funds. For the month as a whole, sales totaled $292 million, then a near-record for any month—and this amount was actually $170 million *more* than the total value of the shares redeemed. Sales thus provided the money necessary to meet redemptions and the funds were not forced to unload portfolio stocks.

Once again Brooks' article sums up the situation: "Apparently the mutual funds had so much cash on hand that in most cases they could pay off their shareholders without selling substantial amounts of stock. Taken as a group, the funds proved to be so rich and so conservatively managed that they not only could weather the storm but, by happy inadvertence, could do something to decrease its violence."

In 1966 the stock market again took a dive and then recovered. From early February to early October, for example, the Dow Jones Industrial Index fell more than 25 per cent. As the year wore on, mutual fund portfolio managers drew in their horns, switching from common stocks into cash and government securities. This conservative behavior paid off. For while mutual fund shares did fall in value, they fell less, by and large, than the market in general. *The Wall Street Journal* reported, for example, that of the nation's 20 largest funds, three suffered losses slightly more severe than the Index, while fully 17 showed smaller losses than the market as a whole.

In buying and selling securities on behalf of their shareholders, did mutual funds contribute to the instability of the market? A special study was undertaken by the Investment Company Institute to examine the activities of 49 funds between August 15 and September 16, 1966. This month-long period had been marked by a sharp drop in market prices, followed by a substantial recovery. The study found that during the period of sharpest decline, the funds were actually slight net buyers. Later, when the market began climbing upward again, the funds were net sellers. They sold $246.6 million more than they bought.

At the same time, the study also showed that fund shareholders bought more shares during this period than they redeemed, once again contradicting the theory that mutual fund shareholders are a timid lot who retreat in disorder when the news is bad. During the month under study, fund shareholders bought nearly $2 worth of shares for every $1 they redeemed.

Can funds be counted on to serve as a balance wheel in the future? Historically, there are many reasons for believing so. However, the question of market stability is extremely complicated, for mutual funds, as we shall see, represent only a part of a much larger phenomenon—the rising importance of institutional investment.

The years since the end of World War II have seen an increase in the proportion of all stocks held by institutions, as distinct from individual holdings. The growth of pension funds in particular has contributed to this process. Money belonging to millions of American workers is concentrated in pension funds. These funds either engage professional investment managers or invest in mutual funds to obtain the advantages of professional management. In either case, they represent great pools of money invested by institutions rather than by individuals.

Taken together with the investments made by life and other insurance companies, bank trust departments, non-profit institutions such as colleges and hospitals, and mutual funds they form an aggregate of great importance. At the end of 1965 institutional investors held slightly more than 20 per cent of all stocks listed on the New York Stock Exchange. According to D. J. Baum and Ned Stiles in *The Silent Partners,* a study of institutional investment, this proportion will rise significantly. And, they speculate, "there is no reason to assume that the accumulation will stop at 40, 50 or even 60 per cent."

Other experts dispute this rather straight-line projection. It has been pointed out that the rate of growth of pension funds will begin to level off after another decade because the funds will begin paying out more money as workers covered by their plans age and retire.

Nevertheless, the growth of institutional investment is one of the most important economic trends of the past twenty years, and the rise of the mutual funds must be seen as part of this pattern. If the funds have risen to importance in the past decade or two and are still growing, how will they fit into the American scene five, ten, or fifteen years from now? No one can answer this question with certainty. But a number of trends are already visible that are likely to take mutual funds down new paths, and it is to these future possibilities and probabilities that we now turn.

Funds and the Future

Chapter Fourteen

T HE FUTURE is always closer than it looks. In a world in which social and technological change are constantly accelerating, the expected (along with the unexpected) usually arrives ahead of schedule. Nobody can blueprint the future, even the future of a single industry. Yet, bearing in mind that blurred vision is an occupational disease among seers, it remains both fruitful and fascinating to peer ahead.

One service that issues reports on mutual funds has estimated that aggregate assets under the management of the industry will reach $48 billion by 1970—a growth of more than 33 per cent in less than half a decade. And, looking even further into the blue tomorrow, one fund president predicts that by the end of the century the assets of the industry will hit $200 billion. "That," he says, "is a conservative figure."

Still another fund official, speaking before a meeting of the Investment Bankers Association, referred to the "highly favorable long-term economic climate." Citing figures prepared by the Long Range Planning Service of the Stanford Research Institute, he predicted a gross national product exceeding $1 trillion by 1975, as compared with a $700 billion annual rate at present. "These projections also indicate that in 1975 there will be more families capable of saving and, with sharply rising family incomes, more families capable of placing some of their savings in equity investments." This likelihood, he said, will be strengthened by the fact that the cost of living will continue to rise at a rate of 1.5 per cent a year—not enough to upset the economy, but enough to make investment in the stock market attractive as a hedge against inflation.

Today, of all holders of corporate securities, only one in five is a mutual fund shareholder. "This proportion should increase markedly," the fund official explained, "because more *average* investors will be coming into the market, and the mutual fund industry is particularly well equipped to meet the average investor's needs."

These optimistic speculations are in general supported by a summary of mutual fund growth prospects prepared for the Commission on Money and Credit. "The trend in individual and institutional financing is still toward more equity investment," the CMC study declares. Moreover, the fund industry "is in a strong competitive position to offer most economically the basic investment advantages of diversification and professional management. . . . The industry has developed many investment service features not readily available in other investment media."

Of course, war or some economic catastrophe could knock all these happy prognostications into a cocked derby. But, barring these and other unforeseen developments, there is widespread agreement that the future for mutual funds looks very bright.

Yet anyone who thinks this over-all growth will occur without painful stress will be in for a shock. Every industry reaches a point in its maturation when further movement upward must be matched by development outward, so to speak. Further increases in the size of the industry must, in other words, bring about changes in methods of operation, elaboration of functions, and greatly increased competition.

Let us look at some of these changes and the impact they are likely to have on mutual funds.

1. *A step-up in competition.* It seems certain that the expanding market for investment services will further intensify competition. Mutual funds will not only have to compete with one another, but also against increasing numbers of firms coming into the industry from without. Competition will be intensified on an inter- as well as an intra-industry level.

Life insurance companies, for example, are well aware that a mutual fund investment and an insurance policy complement one another. Some insurance companies have already set up or acquired mutual fund subsidiaries; others plan to enter the field and offer shares for sale through their army of agents.

Conversely, a number of fund sponsors have gone into the life insurance business on the plausible theory that their salesmen can sell both fund shares and insurance, and that mutual fund investment experts can also manage an insurance company's portfolio. Today the largest mutual fund of all is sponsored by a company that, in addition, manages a $2 billion life insurance operation.

Says one executive whose company straddles both fields: "Everything is moving toward a convergence of insurance and mutual funds. You've got one-stop shopping. Here's one-stop financial and insurance service."

So large does the mutual fund industry potential seem that a variety of companies having little if anything to do with finance have begun to move in, either by buying up existing mutual fund sponsor companies or by planning to sponsor funds of their own. International Telephone and Telegraph has bought control of a management company (an adviser) that services funds with assets of $400 million. The Gates Rubber Company, Kansas City Southern Industries, Inc., and the DuPont-owned Delaware Chemical and Engineering Company have all purchased controlling interests in sponsor firms. And Sears, Roebuck & Co., which already operates a nationwide insurance company, Allstate, has given serious consideration to launching its own mutual fund. If launched, the Sears fund would presumably be sold by Allstate's nearly 5000 insurance agents.

In short, the battle for the investor's dollar will become much more fierce.

2. *Changes in sales methods.* The move toward personal financial planning will be extended. Salesmen will do much more than sell. Just as computer salesmen today help their clients design entire information systems in order to make a computer sale, so, on another level, will mutual fund salesmen help their clients design overall investment policies. The mutual fund salesman, who may also be trained as an insurance salesman, will increasingly serve as financial counselor to his customers, advising them not merely on mutual fund matters, but on insurance and other aspects of financial planning. Selling mutual funds will become an even more systematic and sophisticated procedure than it is today. Salesmen will offer an integrated line of financial services.

3. *Changes in research and portfolio supervision.* The advantage of professional management vis-à-vis do-it-yourself investment will increase sharply. Mutual funds, banks, and other financial institutions are beginning to make more and more sophisticated use of the computer as a tool for portfolio analysis. Conceptual breakthroughs will come along with the gleaming new hardware. Although the computer may never take the place of human judgment in an investment situation, there is little doubt that its careful and intelligent use can be enormously helpful.

Consequently, financial research methods will change. Data will be far more refined and quantified than at present. Investment research will take on a far more mathematical complexion. Probability theory will come into play in the prediction of earnings, dividends, and growth of companies represented in fund portfolios.

As the character of American industry changes under the hammer blows of the technological revolution, financial researchers will have to become far more scientifically and technically knowledgeable in order to ask the right questions of the companies they visit. It may be that, in addition to employing economists and statisticians, mutual funds will increasingly employ operations researchers, mathematicians, behavioral scientists, systems analysts, and other such specialists to back up the financial analysts in their quest for valuable data about portfolio companies.

In brief, just as selling activity will become increasingly systematic, the job of collecting and evaluating information will be done with greater scientific precision.

Mutual fund managers will have better and more precise data on which to base investment decisions, and these

data will be so superior to that available to the average
individual who invests in the market on his own that the
advantage of professional management will be further
dramatized.

Changes such as these will transform the methods used
by mutual funds and the business environment within
which they operate. There will also be great changes in
the reasons *why* people invest. People may buy mutual
fund shares not merely to provide their children with an
education, as they do today, but to provide themselves
with a second college education late in life. They may
invest not to help eke out a marginal living after retirement, as many do today, but to make possible a far more
comfortable standard of living and a wide range of educational and recreational choices.

But, despite all these possible developments, it is unlikely that the central idea on which mutual funds are
based will change soon. The idea of pooling one's money
with others' and purchasing professional management and
diversification will make even more sense in the years
ahead than it does now.

Mutual fund investment will not supplant other types
of saving or investment. Funds are not—and never will
be—a panacea for all investors. Nor is there in the fore-
seeable future any way to eliminate the element of risk
from investment in securities. Investment in stocks and
bonds, either directly or through mutual funds, will therefore remain only part of any well-planned financial program.

Yet it is clear that over the long pull the mutual fund
idea, having already decisively demonstrated its useful-

ness and viability, will continue to gain friends, for the mutual fund concept is sensible, it is adaptable. More important, it is basically attuned to the needs of a mass society moving rapidly into an age of affluence unprecedented in the annals of man.

Bibliography

1. Bullock, Hugh. *The Story of Investment Companies.* New York: Columbia University Press, 1960.
2. Casey, William J. *How to Build Personal and Family Security Out of Your Present Income.* New York: Institute for Business Planning, Inc., 1957.
3. Casey, William J. *Mutual Funds and How to Use Them.* New York: Institute for Business Planning, Inc., 1958.
4. Editors of *Fortune. Fortune's Guide to Personal Investing.* New York: McGraw-Hill, 1963.
5. Engel, Louis. *How to Buy Stocks.* New York: Bantam Books, 1962.
6. Furst, Sidney and Sherman, Milton. *Business Decisions That Changed Our Lives.* New York: Random House, 1964.
7. Johnson, Hugh A. *Making Money With Mutual Funds.* Buffalo, N.Y.: Henry Stewart, Inc., 1955.
8. Jordan, David F. and Dougall, Herbert E. *Investments.* Englewood Cliffs, N.J.: Prentice-Hall, 1964.
9. Knowlton, Winthrop. *Growth Opportunities in Common Stock.* New York: Harper & Row, 1965.
10. Margolius, Sidney. *Your Guide to Financial Security.* New York: The New American Library, 1955.
11. Rauch, Basil. *The History of the New Deal.* New York: Creative Age Press, Inc., 1944.
12. Stabler, C. Norman. *How to Read the Financial News.* New York: Harper & Brothers, 1960.

Reports and Studies

13. *A Comprehensive Study—The Mutual Fund Shareholder.* New York: Investment Company Institute, 1966.
14. *A Study of Mutual Funds,* prepared for the Securities and Exchange Commission by the Wharton School of Finance

and Commerce. Report of the Committee on Interstate and Foreign Commerce, U.S. House of Representatives. House Report Number 2274, 87th Congress, 2nd Session, 1962.

15. *Changing Patterns in Corporate Finance.* By G. Keith Funston, New York Stock Exchange, 1965.

16. *Guide to Business Standards.* New York: Investment Company Institute [n.d.].

17. *Institutional Shareownership.* A research report by the New York Stock Exchange, June 1964.

18. *Investment Company Shares.* By Alec Brock Stevenson. New York: Fiduciary Publishers, Inc., 1947.

19. *Management Investment Companies.* A monograph prepared for the Commission on Money and Credit by the Investment Company Institute. Englewood Cliffs, N.J., Prentice-Hall, 1962.

20. *Mutual Funds, a statistical summary, 1940–1963.* New York: Investment Company Institute, 1964.

21. *Presentation by the Association of Mutual Fund Sponsors, Inc.,* to the Securities and Exchange Commission, February 27, 1964.

22. *Private Capital Markets.* A series of research studies prepared for the Commission on Money and Credit. Englewood Cliffs, N.J.: Prentice-Hall, 1964.

23. *Private Financial Institutions.* A series of research studies prepared for the Commission on Money and Credit. Englewood Cliffs, N.J.: Prentice-Hall, 1963.

24. *Report of the Special Study of Securities Markets of the Securities and Exchange Commission.* House Document Number 95, Part 4, 88th Congress, 1st Session, 1963.

25. *Shareownership USA—1965 Census of Shareowners.* New York Stock Exchange, 1965.

26. *Statistics on the Savings Market,* prepared by Department of Economics and Research, American Bankers Association, 1964.

27. *Survey on Knowledge of and Attitudes toward Mutual Funds,* conducted by Benson & Benson, Inc., for the Investment Company Institute, Princeton, N.J., 1962.
28. *The Investment Outlook, 1964.* Economics Department, Bankers Trust Company, New York, 1964.
29. *The Stock Market under Stress.* Report on the events of May 28, 29, and 31, 1962 by the New York Stock Exchange, March 1963.
30. *What You Must Know. . . . ,* National Association of Securities Dealers, Inc., 1959.

Periodicals

31. "A New Tool in Investment Decision-Making," *Financial Analysts Journal,* May–June 1963, p. 55.
32. "Annals of Finance," *The New Yorker,* August 31, 1963, p. 35.
33. "A Study of Mutual Funds" (review), *American Economic Review,* March 1964, p. 198.
34. "Black, White and Green," *Commercial and Financial Chronicle,* August 20, 1964.
35. "Buy Fund Shares in Supermarkets?" *U.S. News and World Report,* December 9, 1963, p. 120.
36. "Europe's Mushrooming Mutuals," *Time,* January 5, 1962, p. 57.
37. "Funds Again Merging with Holding Groups," *Business Week,* May 9, 1964, p. 109.
38. "Funds in Ferment," *Fortune,* November 1963, p. 247.
39. "Gains, But Not Up to Averages," *Business Week,* January 11, 1964, p. 82.
40. "Get Experts to Help You Invest?" *Changing Times,* May 1964, p. 7.
41. "Getting Comfortable," *Time,* December 18, 1964, p. 77.
42. "Gourmet's Mutual," *Newsweek,* April 30, 1962, p. 78.
43. "Growing Rewards for Prudent Money," *Fortune,* October 1961, p. 136.

44. "How Good Are Mutual Funds," *Fortune*, June 1960, p. 144.

45. "How the Funds Are Faring," *Time*, October 25, 1963, p. 93.

46. "How to Rate Management of Investment Funds," *Harvard Business Review*, January 1965, p. 63.

47. "Investor Withdrawal Plan Sales Spurting," *Wall Street Journal*, September 9, 1964.

48. "Investments: Is the Front-end Load Fair?" *Changing Times*, April 1960, p. 7.

49. "Israel Fund Formed," New York *Herald Tribune*, May 11, 1964.

50. "I.T. & T. Makes Bid for Fund Manager," *The New York Times*, June 14, 1965.

51. "NEA Mutual Fund," *NEA Journal*, November 1964, p. 29.

52. "Never Too Early to Save for Retirement," *Philadelphia Inquirer*, October 18, 1964.

53. "Not So Eager to Plunge," *Business Week*, November 14, 1964, p. 174.

54. "On the Ground Floor," *Newsweek*, May 30, 1955, p. 64.

55. "Only a Trillion," *Newsweek*, July 31, 1961, p. 69.

56. "Outcomes for 'Random' Investments . . . ," *Journal of Business of the University of Chicago*, April 1965.

57. "Performance of Common Trust Funds," *Trusts and Estates*, September 1960, p. 826.

58. "Personal Business," *Business Week*, February 27, 1965, March 20, 1965, p. 151.

59. "Personal Finance: Mutual Funds Optimistic," *The New York Times*, July 6, 1964.

60. "Playing It Safe but Profitably," *Business Week*, August 8, 1964, p. 72.

61. "Profiles," *The New Yorker*, March 8, 1958, p. 47.

62. "Redemptions: Why and What For?" *San Francisco Examiner*, March 12, 1965.

63. "Role of Institutional Investor Studied," *The New York Times,* July 11, 1965.
64. "Sears Is Set to Enter Mutual Fund Race," *Business Week,* February 15, 1964, p. 112.
65. "Stocks the Big Funds Are Buying Now," *U.S. News and World Report,* June 8, 1964, p. 93.
66. "The Profitable Piece Corps," *Time,* August 17, 1962, p. 74.
67. "Those Mysterious No Load Funds," *Dun's Review,* May 1961, p. 42.
68. "What to Do with $1,000,000,000,000," *Fortune,* September 1961, p. 104.

See also:

Annual reports of the Investment Company Institute and of individual mutual funds.

FundScope—monthly published by FundScope, Los Angeles, California; see especially April Mutual Fund Guide.

Institutions and the Stock Market—newsletter published by the New York Stock Exchange.

Investment Companies—annually published by Arthur Wiesenberger & Co., New York.

Investment Company Newsletter—monthly published by the Investment Company Institute.

Investment Dealers' Digest—weekly published by Dealer's Digest Publishing Co., New York; see especially Mutual Fund Directory issue.

Johnson's Investment Company Charts—annually published by Hugh Johnson & Co., Buffalo, New York.

Mutual Affairs—newsletter published by Arthur Wiesenberger & Co., New York.

Mutual Funds—annual statistical summary issued by Investment Company Institute, New York.

Index

Accumulation plan, 38–39, 53
  linked to life insurance, 43
Advantages of mutual funds, three
  key, 8–9
Adviser, mutual fund (*see* Management, mutual fund)
Allstate, 132
AMA (*see* American Medical Association)
American Council on Education, 15
American Medical Association, 15
American Telephone & Telegraph,
  33, 63
Ampex, 94
Assets, net value per share of
  mutual fund, 23
A.T.&T. (*see* American Telephone
  & Telegraph)
Automatic reinvestment plan, 43
Averages, stock market, 60–63, 81,
  120, 126
Aztec Oil & Gas Co., 34

Balanced fund, 31, 36–37
Barron's, 67, 82
Baum, D. J., 128
Beech Aircraft Corp., 34
Bond-and-preferred stock funds,
  30–31, 59–60
Bonds, 7
Brooks, John, 10, 120, 124–126
Budget Bureau, 79
Burroughs, 94
Business Week, 16

Capital appreciation fund, 33–34
Capital gains, 10, 24–26, 38–39,
  42
  tax on, 25
  long-term, 25

Capital, growth of, 30
Casey, William J., 14–15
Cash reserves needed by mutual
  funds, 25
Center for Research in Security
  Prices, University of Chicago,
  60
Classification of mutual funds, 30–
  34
Closed-end investment companies,
  9, 21
  defined, 9
  assets as of December 31, 1966,
  9
Collateral, 43
College Entrance Examination
  Boards, 15
Columbia Broadcasting, 34
Commercial and Financial Chronicle, 122
Commission on Money and Credit,
  37, 58, 122, 130
Commissions, mutual fund, 45–55,
  104–105
Common stock funds, 33–35
Common stocks, 6, 12–13, 31–32
Compound interest, 3
Computer analysis, 81, 133
Computers, 81, 99, 100, 133
Contractual investment plan, 38–
  39, 53–54
Conversion privilege, 41
Corporate securities, 7
Costs of mutual fund services, 45–
  55
  management fee, 46–47, 53, 55
  operating expenses, 47–48
  sales charge, 48–55

[143]

Depression, mutual fund compared with direct investments during, 57

Diversification in mutual fund portfolio, 9, 26–27, 51

Dividend reinvestment account, 38

Dividends
as criteria for judging investment progress, 24
distributed by mutual funds in 1966, 10
reinvestment of, 38–39
tax on, 25

Dollar cost averaging, 39–40

Dow-Jones Average (*see* Dow-Jones Industrial Stock Average)

Dow-Jones Industrial Index (*see* Dow-Jones Industrial Stock Average)

Dow-Jones Industrial Stock Average, 62–63, 81, 120, 126

Doyle, William, 9

Dun's Review, 105

Dupont (*see* Delaware Chemical and Engineering Company)

Eastman Kodak, 34

Education, cost of, 15–16

Engel, Louis, 123–124

Equity funds (*see* Common stock funds)

Exchange funds, 42

Fairchild Camera, 94

Federal laws governing mutual funds, 76–77, 111–118

Federal Reserve Board, 79

Federal Reserve Bulletin, 79

Federal Securities Act of 1933, 112

Federal Securities Exchange Act of 1934, 112

Flexibility of mutual funds, 37

Forbes, 67

Fortune, 4–5, 68–69, 116–118

Fractional shares, 63

Front-end load (*see* Contractual investment plan)

FundScope, 67

Fund-rating publications, 66–67

Funston, G. Keith, 121

Gates Rubber Company, 132

General Electric, 33

General Motors, 8, 33

Government bonds, low-interest, 4

Growth, investment
criteria for judging, 24–25
time as a factor in, 57–58

Growth funds, 33–34

Growth potential
in bank deposits, 5
in life insurance, 5–6
in mutual fund investment, 56–58

Growth, mutual fund industry's future, 129–135

Growth Opportunities in Common Stocks, 64

Guide to Business Standards, 111, 119

How to Buy Stocks, 123–124

Humphrey, Hubert, 13

IBM, 34, 94
IBM 1401, 100
IBM 1410, 100

Income (*see* Investment income)

Inflation, 6, 14, 18

Institutional accounts holding mutual fund shares, 127–128

Inflation, 6, 14, 18

Institutional accounts holding mutual fund shares, 127–128
size of, 18
types of, 17–19

Institutional investment, 127–128

Internal Revenue Code, 25, 111–112

International Business Machines (*see* IBM)

International Telephone and Telegraph, 132

Investment Bankers Association, 129

Investment Companies, 50–51, 66, 111

Investment Company Act of 1940, 77, 114–116

Investment Company Institute, 6, 13–14, 18, 111, 119, 126–127

Investment counsellor, 28–29, 46–47

Investment Dealer's Digest (*see* *Mutual Fund Directory*)

Investment growth
criteria for judging, 24–25
time as a factor in, 57–58

Investment income, 25, 30

Investment media, 4–8

Investment objectives of mutual funds
as a means of rating performance, 59–60
three basic, 30–35

Investment plans, types of, 38

Investment policy, 87–91

Investments, 57

Investments
four chief media for American, 5–8
ideal, definition of, 5
mutual fund
long-term, value of, 57–58

Investments (*Cont.*)
mutual fund (*Cont.*)
performance compared with direct investments, 56–57

Investors in mutual funds (*see* Shareholders, mutual fund)

Itek Corp., 34

Johnson's Charts, 66

Johnson, Hugh & Co., Inc. (*see* *Johnson's Charts*)

Kansas City Southern Industries, Inc., 132

Knowlton, Winthrop, 64

Labor unions, mutual fund holdings of, 18

Laws
governing commissions on contractual plans, 53–54
governing mutual funds, 76–77, 111–118
governing mutual fund presentation of performance, 68

Letter of intent, 48–49

Life insurance, 4–6, 43, 54, 131

Liquidity, mutual fund, 8–9, 27

Litho Color Plate Company, 17

Long Range Planning Service of the Stanford Research Institute, 129–130

Long-term gains, 34

Low-interest government bonds, 4

Management fee, 46–47, 53, 55

Management Investment Companies, 37

Management, mutual fund, 46–47, 74–77

Marcus, Professor Edward, 122–123

Measurement of mutual fund performance, 67–68
Metromedia, Inc., 34
Mobil Oil Corporation, 17
Monthly Investment Plan, New York Stock Exchange, 50
Moon, Rexford, G., 15–16
Mutual Fund Directory of the *Investment Dealer's Digest*, 66–68
   typical listing in, 67
Mutual funds
   definition of, 21
   growth of industry, 9–10
   history, 10, 29
   institutional investments in, 17–18
   legal entity, 75
   payments to shareholders in 1966, 10
   sale of share in 1966, 10
   services, 36–43
   size of individual holdings in, 16–17
   types of, 29–35
   variety of, 29–34
Mutual funds, operation of
   administration, 98–102
   investment policymaking, 87–91
   portfolio activities, 91–97
   research, 73–86, 133–134

National Association of Securities Dealers, 107, 117
Net asset value, 23–25
New York Stock Exchange, 60, 120–121, 125–128
   average price of a stock on the, 51
   Monthly Investment Plan, 50
New York Stock Exchange Commission rates, 50
The New York Times, 82

The New Yorker, 10, 120
No-load funds, 52–53

Objectives (*see* Investment objectives of mutual funds)
Odd-lot commissions, 51–52, 63
Open-end investment company (*see* Mutual funds)
Open-end investment trust (*see* Mutual funds)

Pension funds, 17–18
Performance of mutual funds, 56–69
   measurement of, 67–68
Periodicals reporting on mutual funds, 66–67
Preferred stocks (*see* Bond-and-preferred stock funds)
Price of mutual fund share, determination of, 23
Private Financial Institutions, 58, 122
Professional investment counselor (*see* Investment counselor)
Prospectus of mutual fund, content of, 26
Publications, fund-rating, 66–67

Redemption, 25–26, 40, 45, 49–50, 108, 123–127
Reinvestment, of dividends, of capital-gains distributions, 60–61
Retirement, 13–15
Richardson, Dorsey, 6
Risk-reward spectrum, ranging mutual funds on a, 34–35
Roosevelt, Franklin Delano, 56
Round-lot commissions, 51–52

St. John's University (Minn.), 18–19

Sale of mutual fund shares, mechanism for, 103–108
Sales charge on mutual funds (*see* Commissions, mutual fund)
Savings deposits, 5
Sears, Roebuck & Co., 132
SEC (*see* Securities and Exchange Commission)
Securities and Exchange Commission, 105, 107, 111, 113–118
Services, mutual fund, 45–55, 98–102
Shareholders, mutual fund, 12–20
  institutional, 17–20
  length of time they hold shares, 57–58
  reasons for investing, 13–16
The Silent Partners, 128
Soukup, Rev. Gervase J., 18–19
Sponsor (*see* Management, mutual fund)
Standard and Poor's 500 Stock Index, 60–61, 63, 81
Stanford Research Institute, Long Range Planning Service of the, 129–130
Statements from mutual funds, periodic, 25–26
Stiles, Ned, 128
Stock market, 6, 33
Stock prices, 60–61
Stock splits, 62–63
Stocks, publicly traded
  number of owners in 1966, 6

Survey of Current Business of the Department of Commerce, 79
Survey Research Center of the University of Michigan, 13–14
Systematic redemption program, 39–40

Tax characteristics of mutual funds, 25
Tax Foundation, 79
Texas Instruments, 94
Treasury Department, 79
Trusts, 42–43
Trusts and Estates, 67

United States Steel, 22
University of Chicago Center for Research in Security Prices, 60

Voluntary investment plan, 38–39

The Wall Street Journal, 41, 47, 82, 126
Wesner, Charles P., 17
Wharton Report, 60–61
Wiesenberger, Arthur & Co., 8, 50, 51, 66 (*see also Investment Companies*)
Withdrawal account (*see* Systematic redemption program)
Woolworth, F. W., 63

Xerox, 94